Psalm 83 and Isai

Heather L. Rivard

Table of Contents

An Introduction to Psalm 83

In these last days, many people have become aware of the upcoming Battle of Gog and Magog, as referenced in Ezekiel 38-39. Perhaps even more well-known than the Battle of Gog and Magog is the Battle of Armageddon, referenced in Revelation 16 and 19. There is another passage of scripture to which attention has been drawn in recent years: Psalm 83.

There are opposing viewpoints about Psalm 83 and whether it regards an altogether different battle than Gog and Magog or Armageddon. Some believe it is separate and distinct from those two, further supposing Psalm 83 will occur before both Gog and Magog and Armageddon. The purpose of this study is to see what the Bible says about the timing of Psalm 83. We will begin by looking at the text of Psalm 83.

> *Psalm 83:1 Keep not thou silence, O God: hold not thy peace, and be not still, O God. 2 For, lo, thine enemies make a tumult: and they that hate thee have lifted up the head. 3 They have taken crafty counsel against thy people, and consulted against thy hidden ones. 4 They have said, Come, and let us cut them off from being a nation; that the name of Israel may be no more in remembrance. 5 For they have consulted together with one consent: they are confederate against thee: 6 The tabernacles of Edom, and the Ishmaelites; of Moab, and the Hagarenes; 7 Gebal, and Ammon, and Amalek; the Philistines with the inhabitants of Tyre; 8 Assur also is joined with them: they have holpen the children of Lot. Selah. 9 Do unto them as unto the Midianites; as to Sisera, as to Jabin, at the brook of Kison: 10 Which perished at Endor: they became as dung for the earth. 11 Make their nobles like Oreb, and like Zeeb: yea, all their princes as Zebah, and as Zalmunna: 12 Who said, Let us take to ourselves the houses of God in possession. 13 O my God, make them like a wheel; as the stubble before the wind. 14 As the fire burneth a wood, and as the flame setteth the mountains on fire; 15 So persecute them with thy tempest,*

and make them afraid with thy storm. 16 Fill their faces with shame; that they may seek thy name, O LORD. 17 Let them be confounded and troubled for ever; yea, let them be put to shame, and perish: 18 That men may know that thou, whose name alone is JEHOVAH, art the most high over all the earth.[1]

Psalm 83 is referred to as an imprecatory prayer and was written by Asaph, a "seer" and leader of David's choir.[2] Imprecatory means "to invoke or call down (evil or curses), as upon a person".[3] Much of the debate surrounding this chapter stems from whether God will respond to this prayer, and if so, when He will respond. Will it be before, during, or after Daniel's 70th Week? Will it be before the Battle of Gog and Magog and Armageddon, or will it be in conjunction with one of those battles? To answer those questions, we need to break down each verse of the chapter so we know exactly what we are dealing with.

To make this study a bit easier, I will break Psalm 83 down into four sections. The first section will deal with verses 1-5 which establish intent. The second section will define the people groups involved as named in verses 6-8. The third section will include verses 9-12 which detail Israel's God-given victories over specific enemies. The final section will discuss verses 13-18 which give us a bit different insight. You will see what I mean when we get there. Let's begin with Psalm 83:1-5.

Psalm 83:1-5

Psalm 83:1 Keep not thou silence, O God: hold not thy peace, and be not still, O God. 2 For, lo, thine enemies make a tumult: and they that hate thee have lifted up the head. 3 They have taken crafty counsel against thy people, and consulted against thy hidden ones. 4 They have said, Come, and let us cut them off from being a nation; that the name of Israel may be no more in remembrance. 5 For they have consulted together with one consent: they are confederate against thee:

The first thing this prayer does is ask God to act. That He is being asked to not keep His silence, hold not His peace, and be not still infers that He is currently silent, peaceful, and still regarding these people groups. Perhaps it is not so much that He is peaceful with them so much as He is not actively at war with them. This distinction will become important in later sections. We are then given the reasons why God is being implored to act.

It is extremely important to note these enemies are not primarily enemies of Israel's. They are enemies of God's. Because of their stance against God, they are attempting to get to God through the only means they have: His people Israel. Thus, we are told they have taken crafty counsel against "thy people" and consulted against "thy hidden ones".

There is a secondary debate within the Bible prophecy community about who is intended of "thy people" and "thy hidden ones". Some believe it is a veiled reference to the church who will be hidden in heaven during the whole of Daniel's 70th Week. This viewpoint is easily disputed by the text of Psalm 83:4 which states the intent of this people group is to cut Israel off from being a nation that her name be remembered no more. Thus, we should not infer the church is intended. Furthermore, even if all members of the church died, they would still be in heaven with Jesus.

> *I Corinthians 5:8 We are confident, I say, and willing rather to be absent from the body, and to be present with the Lord.[4]*

Thus, eliminating the church would not achieve the desired outcome of these people groups. However, to their way of thinking, eliminating the nation of Israel would achieve such an outcome. It should be understood they do not desire to wipe the land area of Israel off the map. Rather, they desire to eliminate all the people who belong to the nation of Israel. This speaks to the larger issue at hand, an issue which began with the first prophecy in the Garden of Eden.

> *Genesis 3:15 And I will put enmity between thee and the woman, and between thy seed and her seed; it shall bruise thy head, and thou shalt bruise his heel.*[5]

From the time sin entered the world at the hand of the deceiving serpent, Satan's time in this world was given an expiration date. Through the lineage of Eve, a Messiah would be born who would eternally defeat Satan. For this reason, Abel was killed. At the time, Satan was unaware Adam and Eve would have other offspring. Even so, it would be from the line of a different child that Messiah would come. Genesis 5 tells us from the lineage of Seth came Noah. After the flood, Abraham descended from the line of Shem, one of Noah's three sons. Matthew 1 gives us Jesus's direct lineage from Abraham. Thus, the seed of the woman came from Seth and Noah and Shem and Abraham. It will be Jesus Christ who will crush the head of Satan. This very prophecy is what Satan has continued to attempt to thwart since the very beginning.

Throughout the stories in the Old Testament, regardless of what ill Israel suffered because of her apostasy, God has always preserved a remnant. We see this in the story of Elijah and the Israelites who worshipped Baal in I Kings 19.

> *I Kings 19:14 And he said, I have been very jealous for the LORD God of hosts: because the children of Israel have forsaken thy covenant, thrown down thine altars, and slain thy prophets with the sword; and I, even I only, am left; and they seek my life, to take it away. 15 And the LORD said unto him, Go, return on thy way to the wilderness of Damascus: and when thou comest, anoint Hazael to be king over Syria:*

16 And Jehu the son of Nimshi shalt thou anoint to be king over Israel: and Elisha the son of Shaphat of Abelmeholah shalt thou anoint to be prophet in thy room. 17 And it shall come to pass, that him that escapeth the sword of Hazael shall Jehu slay: and him that escapeth from the sword of Jehu shall Elisha slay. 18 Yet I have left me seven thousand in Israel, all the knees which have not bowed unto Baal, and every mouth which hath not kissed him.

We see this in Ezra 2 when the Israelites returned from the Babylonian Captivity.

Ezra 2:64 The whole congregation together was forty and two thousand three hundred and threescore, 65 Beside their servants and their maids, of whom there were seven thousand three hundred thirty and seven: and there were among them two hundred singing men and singing women. 66 Their horses were seven hundred thirty and six; their mules, two hundred forty and five; 67 Their camels, four hundred thirty and five; their asses, six thousand seven hundred and twenty. 68 And some of the chief of the fathers, when they came to the house of the LORD which is at Jerusalem, offered freely for the house of God to set it up in his place: 69 They gave after their ability unto the treasure of the work threescore and one thousand drams of gold, and five thousand pound of silver, and one hundred priests' garments. 70 So the priests, and the Levites, and some of the people, and the singers, and the porters, and the Nethinims, dwelt in their cities, and all Israel in their cities. [6]

We see this in Ezekiel 37's "dry bones" prophecy, where the land was given back to Israel following the World War II, as reparations for the Holocaust.

Ezekiel 37:1 The hand of the LORD was upon me, and carried me out in the spirit of the LORD, and set me down in the midst of the valley which was full of bones, 2 And caused me to pass by them round about: and, behold, there were very many in the open valley; and, lo, they were very dry. 3 And he said unto me, Son of man, can these bones live? And I answered, O Lord GOD, thou knowest. 4 Again he said unto me, Prophesy upon these bones, and say unto them, O ye dry bones, hear the word of the LORD. 5 Thus saith the Lord GOD unto these bones; Behold, I will cause breath to enter into you, and ye shall live: 6 And I will lay sinews upon you, and will bring up flesh upon you, and cover you with skin, and put breath in you, and ye shall live; and ye shall know that I am the LORD. 7 So I prophesied as I was commanded: and as I prophesied, there was a noise, and behold a shaking, and the bones came together, bone to his bone. 8 And when I beheld, lo, the sinews and the flesh came up upon them, and the skin covered them above: but there was no breath in them. 9 Then said he unto me, Prophesy unto the wind, prophesy, son of man, and say to the wind, Thus saith the Lord GOD; Come from the four winds, O breath, and breathe upon these slain, that they may live. 10 So I prophesied as he commanded me, and the breath came into them, and they lived, and stood up upon their feet, an exceeding great army. 11 Then he said unto me, Son of man, these bones are the whole house of Israel: behold, they say, Our bones are dried, and our hope is lost: we are cut off for our parts. 12 Therefore prophesy and say unto them, Thus saith the Lord GOD; Behold, O my people, I will open your graves, and cause you to come up out of your graves, and bring you into the land of Israel. 13 And ye shall know that I am the LORD, when I have opened your graves, O my people, and brought you up out of your graves, 14 And shall put my spirit in you, and ye shall live, and I shall place you in your own land: then shall ye know that I the LORD have spoken it, and performed it, saith the LORD.[7]

A remnant will also be preserved so they can call Jesus back for His Second Coming.

Joel 2:32 And it shall come to pass, that whosoever shall call on the name of the LORD shall be delivered: for in mount Zion and in Jerusalem shall be deliverance, as the LORD hath said, and in the remnant whom the LORD shall call.[8]

Why has it been important for the Lord to preserve a remnant? So the name of Israel will always be remembered.

The rapture of the church is a foregone conclusion. In John 14:1-3, Jesus promised to return for the church and take them to His Father's house. In Romans 8:30, the church is further given the hope and promise of glorification. This must be done, because I Corinthians 15:50 tells us flesh and blood cannot inherit the kingdom of God.

> *I Corinthians 15:49 And as we have borne the image of the earthy, we shall also bear the image of the heavenly. 50 Now this I say, brethren, that flesh and blood cannot inherit the kingdom of God; neither doth corruption inherit incorruption.*[9]

Since the kingdom of God will at that time still be in heaven, we must be changed before we can be taken there. However, there are a different sequence of steps necessary to bring the Kingdom from heaven to earth. Jesus plainly told the religious leaders of His day they would not see Him again until…

> *Matthew 23:39 For I say unto you, Ye shall not see me henceforth, till ye shall say, Blessed is he that cometh in the name of the Lord.*[10]

Zechariah 13 affirms this statement.

> *Zechariah 13:9 And I will bring the third part through the fire, and will refine them as silver is refined, and will try them as gold is tried: they shall call on my name, and I will hear them: I will say, It is my people: and they shall say, The LORD is my God.*[11]

For a remnant of Israel to be left by the end of Daniel's 70th Week so she can call upon the name of the Lord and precipitate His return, God must preserve them. Thus, Jesus gives the following warning in Matthew 24:

Matthew 24:15 When ye therefore shall see the abomination of desolation, spoken of by Daniel the prophet, stand in the holy place, (whoso readeth, let him understand:) 16 Then let them which be in Judaea flee into the mountains: 17 Let him which is on the housetop not come down to take any thing out of his house: 18 Neither let him which is in the field return back to take his clothes. 19 And woe unto them that are with child, and to them that give suck in those days! 20 But pray ye that your flight be not in the winter, neither on the sabbath day: 21 For then shall be great tribulation, such as was not since the beginning of the world to this time, no, nor ever shall be. 22 And except those days should be shortened, there should no flesh be saved: but for the elect's sake those days shall be shortened.[12]

Presumably, those who do not flee will be killed. While they could be resurrected as martyrs at the end of the Week, the Lord needs live bodies to call Him back. Thus, for the sake of the elect, or as Joel 2:32 puts it, "the remnant the Lord shall call", their time in Jerusalem will be shortened by their flight to Bozrah. Satan does not handle this well.

Revelation 12:12 Therefore rejoice, ye heavens, and ye that dwell in them. Woe to the inhabiters of the earth and of the sea! for the devil is come down unto you, having great wrath, because he knoweth that he hath but a short time. 13 And when the dragon saw that he was cast unto the earth, he persecuted the woman which brought forth the man child. 14 And to the woman were given two wings of a great eagle, that she might fly into the wilderness, into her place, where she is nourished for a time, and times, and half a time, from the face of the serpent. 15 And the serpent cast out of his mouth water as a flood after the woman, that he might cause her to be carried away of the flood. 16 And the earth helped the woman, and the earth opened her mouth, and swallowed up the flood which the dragon cast out of his mouth. 17 And the dragon was wroth with the woman, and went to make war with the remnant of her seed, which keep the commandments of God, and have the testimony of Jesus Christ.[13]

Hopefully, you understand how this all plays into the text of Psalm 83:4.

> *Psalm 83:4 They have said, Come, and let us cut them off from being a nation; that the name of Israel may be no more in remembrance.*

If the enemies of the Lord who target His people were to be successful in eliminating them, the Second Coming would be thwarted. God has always and will always preserve a remnant for this reason. God's prophecy of Satan's demise must be fulfilled. For that to occur, Jesus must return and defeat him. To do that, a remnant must exist to call Him back. See how it's all linked together?

> *Psalm 83:5 For they have consulted together with one consent: they are confederate against thee:*

Who are these people who have lifted up the head, who have consulted together with one consent, and who are confederate against God?

Psalm 83:6-8

Psalm 83:6 The tabernacles of Edom, and the Ishmaelites; of Moab, and the Hagarenes; 7 Gebal, and Ammon, and Amalek; the Philistines with the inhabitants of Tyre; 8 Assur also is joined with them: they have holpen the children of Lot. Selah.

There are 10 people groups listed above: the tabernacles of Edom; the Ishmaelites; the people of Moab; the Hagarenes; the people of Gebal, Ammon, and Amalek; the Philistines; the inhabitants of Tyre; and, Assur. To begin, we need to identify these ancient land areas as they would have been regarded in Asaph's day. Below is a map representing the land areas and people groups named in Psalm 83.

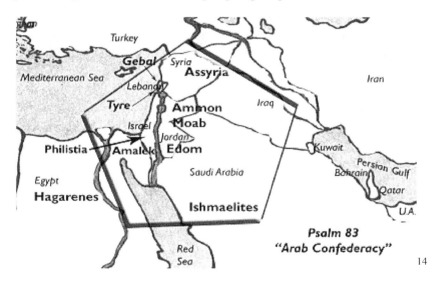

While the proximity of these people groups to Israel is important, perhaps equally as important are their relationships to Israel's progenitors.

Edom = Esau vs. Jacob

> *Genesis 25:29: And Jacob sod pottage: and Esau came from the field, and he was faint: 30 And Esau said to Jacob, Feed me, I pray thee, with that same red pottage; for I am faint:*

*therefore was his name called Edom. 31 And Jacob said, Sell
me this day thy birthright. 32 And Esau said, Behold, I am at
the point to die: and what profit shall this birthright do to
me? 33 And Jacob said, Swear to me this day; and he sware
unto him: and he sold his birthright unto Jacob. 34 Then
Jacob gave Esau bread and pottage of lentiles; and he did
eat and drink, and rose up, and went his way: thus Esau
despised his birthright.[15]*

*Genesis 27:30 And it came to pass, as soon as Isaac had
made an end of blessing Jacob, and Jacob was yet scarce
gone out from the presence of Isaac his father, that Esau his
brother came in from his hunting. 31 And he also had made
savoury meat, and brought it unto his father, and said unto
his father, Let my father arise, and eat of his son's venison,
that thy soul may bless me. 32 And Isaac his father said unto
him, Who art thou? And he said, I am thy son, thy firstborn
Esau. 33 And Isaac trembled very exceedingly, and said,
Who? where is he that hath taken venison, and brought it me,
and I have eaten of all before thou camest, and have blessed
him? yea, and he shall be blessed. 34 And when Esau heard
the words of his father, he cried with a great and exceeding
bitter cry, and said unto his father, Bless me, even me also, O
my father. 35 And he said, Thy brother came with subtilty,
and hath taken away thy blessing. 36 And he said, Is not he
rightly named Jacob? for he hath supplanted me these two
times: he took away my birthright; and, behold, now he hath
taken away my blessing. And he said, Hast thou not reserved
a blessing for me? 37 And Isaac answered and said unto
Esau, Behold, I have made him thy lord, and all his brethren
have I given to him for servants; and with corn and wine
have I sustained him: and what shall I do now unto thee, my
son? 38 And Esau said unto his father, Hast thou but one
blessing, my father? bless me, even me also, O my father.
And Esau lifted up his voice, and wept. 39 And Isaac his
father answered and said unto him, Behold, thy dwelling
shall be the fatness of the earth, and of the dew of heaven
from above; 40 And by thy sword shalt thou live, and shalt
serve thy brother; and it shall come to pass when thou shalt*

have the dominion, that thou shalt break his yoke from off thy neck. 41 And Esau hated Jacob because of the blessing wherewith his father blessed him: and Esau said in his heart, The days of mourning for my father are at hand; then will I slay my brother Jacob.[16]

Amalek = offspring of Esau vs. offspring of Jacob

Genesis 36:15 These were dukes of the sons of Esau: the sons of Eliphaz the firstborn son of Esau; duke Teman, duke Omar, duke Zepho, duke Kenaz, 16 Duke Korah, duke Gatam, and duke Amalek: these are the dukes that came of Eliphaz in the land of Edom; these were the sons of Adah.[17]

Exodus 17:8 Then came Amalek, and fought with Israel in Rephidim. 9 And Moses said unto Joshua, Choose us out men, and go out, fight with Amalek: to morrow I will stand on the top of the hill with the rod of God in mine hand. 10 So Joshua did as Moses had said to him, and fought with Amalek: and Moses, Aaron, and Hur went up to the top of the hill. 11 And it came to pass, when Moses held up his hand, that Israel prevailed: and when he let down his hand, Amalek prevailed. 12 But Moses hands were heavy; and they took a stone, and put it under him, and he sat thereon; and Aaron and Hur stayed up his hands, the one on the one side, and the other on the other side; and his hands were steady until the going down of the sun. 13 And Joshua discomfited Amalek and his people with the edge of the sword. 14 And the LORD said unto Moses, Write this for a memorial in a book, and rehearse it in the ears of Joshua: for I will utterly put out the remembrance of Amalek from under heaven. 15 And Moses built an altar, and called the name of it Jehovahnissi: 16 For he said, Because the LORD hath sworn that the LORD will have war with Amalek from generation to generation.[18]

Ishmaelites and Hagarenes = Ishmael vs. Isaac

Genesis 16:1 Now Sarai Abram's wife bare him no children: and she had an handmaid, an Egyptian, whose name was

14

Hagar. 2 And Sarai said unto Abram, Behold now, the LORD hath restrained me from bearing: I pray thee, go in unto my maid; it may be that I may obtain children by her. And Abram hearkened to the voice of Sarai. 3 And Sarai Abram's wife took Hagar her maid the Egyptian, after Abram had dwelt ten years in the land of Canaan, and gave her to her husband Abram to be his wife. 4 And he went in unto Hagar, and she conceived: and when she saw that she had conceived, her mistress was despised in her eyes. 5 And Sarai said unto Abram, My wrong be upon thee: I have given my maid into thy bosom; and when she saw that she had conceived, I was despised in her eyes: the LORD judge between me and thee. 6 But Abram said unto Sarai, Behold, thy maid is in thine hand; do to her as it pleaseth thee. And when Sarai dealt hardly with her, she fled from her face. 7 And the angel of the LORD found her by a fountain of water in the wilderness, by the fountain in the way to Shur. 8 And he said, Hagar, Sarai's maid, whence camest thou? and whither wilt thou go? And she said, I flee from the face of my mistress Sarai. 9 And the angel of the LORD said unto her, Return to thy mistress, and submit thyself under her hands. 10 And the angel of the LORD said unto her, I will multiply thy seed exceedingly, that it shall not be numbered for multitude. 11 And the angel of the LORD said unto her, Behold, thou art with child and shalt bear a son, and shalt call his name Ishmael; because the LORD hath heard thy affliction. 12 And he will be a wild man; his hand will be against every man, and every man's hand against him; and he shall dwell in the presence of all his brethren. 13 And she called the name of the LORD that spake unto her, Thou God seest me: for she said, Have I also here looked after him that seeth me? 14 Wherefore the well was called Beerlahairoi; behold, it is between Kadesh and Bered. 15 And Hagar bare Abram a son: and Abram called his son's name, which Hagar bare, Ishmael. 16 And Abram was fourscore and six years old, when Hagar bare Ishmael to Abram.[19]

Genesis 17:15 And God said unto Abraham, As for Sarai thy wife, thou shalt not call her name Sarai, but Sarah shall her name be. 16 And I will bless her, and give thee a son also of her: yea, I will bless her, and she shall be a mother of nations; kings of people shall be of her. 17 Then Abraham fell upon his face, and laughed, and said in his heart, Shall a child be born unto him that is an hundred years old? and shall Sarah, that is ninety years old, bear? 18 And Abraham said unto God, O that Ishmael might live before thee! 19 And God said, Sarah thy wife shall bear thee a son indeed; and thou shalt call his name Isaac: and I will establish my covenant with him for an everlasting covenant, and with his seed after him. 20 And as for Ishmael, I have heard thee: Behold, I have blessed him, and will make him fruitful, and will multiply him exceedingly; twelve princes shall he beget, and I will make him a great nation. 21 But my covenant will I establish with Isaac, which Sarah shall bear unto thee at this set time in the next year.[20]

Moab and Ammon = offspring of Lot vs. offspring of Abraham

Genesis 19:27 And Abraham gat up early in the morning to the place where he stood before the LORD: 28 And he looked toward Sodom and Gomorrah, and toward all the land of the plain, and beheld, and, lo, the smoke of the country went up as the smoke of a furnace. 29 And it came to pass, when God destroyed the cities of the plain, that God remembered Abraham, and sent Lot out of the midst of the overthrow, when he overthrew the cities in the which Lot dwelt. 30 And Lot went up out of Zoar, and dwelt in the mountain, and his two daughters with him; for he feared to dwell in Zoar: and he dwelt in a cave, he and his two daughters. 31 And the firstborn said unto the younger, Our father is old, and there is not a man in the earth to come in unto us after the manner of all the earth: 32 Come, let us make our father drink wine, and we will lie with him, that we may preserve seed of our father. 33 And they made their father drink wine that night: and the firstborn went in, and lay with her father; and he perceived not when she lay down, nor when she arose. 34 And it came to pass on the morrow, that the firstborn said unto the younger, Behold, I lay yesternight with my father: let

*us make him drink wine this night also; and go thou in, and
lie with him, that we may preserve seed of our father. 35 And
they made their father drink wine that night also: and the
younger arose, and lay with him; and he perceived not when
she lay down, nor when she arose. 36 Thus were both the
daughters of Lot with child by their father. 37 And the first
born bare a son, and called his name Moab: the same is the
father of the Moabites unto this day. 38 And the younger, she
also bare a son, and called his name Benammi: the same is
the father of the children of Ammon unto this day.*[21]

Philistines = the line of Ham vs. the line of Shem

*Genesis 10:6 And the sons of Ham; Cush, and Mizraim, and
Phut, and Canaan. 7 And the sons of Cush; Seba, and
Havilah, and Sabtah, and Raamah, and Sabtechah: and the
sons of Raamah; Sheba, and Dedan. 8 And Cush begat
Nimrod: he began to be a mighty one in the earth. 9 He was a
mighty hunter before the LORD: wherefore it is said, Even as
Nimrod the mighty hunter before the LORD. 10 And the
beginning of his kingdom was Babel, and Erech, and Accad,
and Calneh, in the land of Shinar. 11 Out of that land went
forth Asshur, and builded Nineveh, and the city Rehoboth,
and Calah, 12 And Resen between Nineveh and Calah: the
same is a great city. 13 And Mizraim begat Ludim, and
Anamim, and Lehabim, and Naphtuhim, 14 And Pathrusim,
and <u>Casluhim, (out of whom came Philistim,)</u> and
Caphtorim.*[22]

When God was giving Moses instructions for taking possession of
the Promised Land, He said the following:

*Exodus 23:31 And I will set thy bounds from the Red sea even
unto the sea of the Philistines, and from the desert unto the
river: for I will deliver the inhabitants of the land into your
hand; and thou shalt drive them out before thee.*[23]

However, Israel did not do as the Lord commanded. We find account
of this in Joshua 13. Thus, they were destined for perpetual war with

the Philistines.[24] The same applies to Gebal, being descended of Edom and Esau, as they are also mentioned in Joshua 13:5.

> *Joshua 13:1 Now Joshua was old and stricken in years; and the LORD said unto him, Thou art old and stricken in years, and there remaineth yet very much land to be possessed. 2 This is the land that yet remaineth: all the borders of the Philistines, and all Geshuri, 3 From Sihor, which is before Egypt, even unto the borders of Ekron northward, which is counted to the Canaanite: five lords of the Philistines; the Gazathites, and the Ashdothites, the Eshkalonites, the Gittites, and the Ekronites; also the Avites: 4 From the south, all the land of the Canaanites, and Mearah that is beside the Sidonians unto Aphek, to the borders of the Amorites: 5 And the land of the Giblites, and all Lebanon, toward the sunrising, from Baalgad under mount Hermon unto the entering into Hamath.[25]*

Thus, **Gebal = the line of Esau vs. the line of Jacob**

Tyre = the line of Esau vs. the line of Jacob

> *Amos 1:9 Thus saith the LORD; For three transgressions of Tyrus, and for four, I will not turn away the punishment thereof; because they delivered up the whole captivity to Edom, and remembered not the brotherly covenant: 10 But I will send a fire on the wall of Tyrus, which shall devour the palaces thereof.[26]*

Assur (Assyrians) = the line of Ham vs. the line of Shem

> *Genesis 10:6 And the sons of Ham; Cush, and Mizraim, and Phut, and Canaan. 7 And the sons of Cush; Seba, and Havilah, and Sabtah, and Raamah, and Sabtechah: and the sons of Raamah; Sheba, and Dedan. 8 And Cush begat Nimrod: he began to be a mighty one in the earth. 9 He was a mighty hunter before the LORD: wherefore it is said, Even as Nimrod the mighty hunter before the LORD. 10 And the beginning of his kingdom was Babel, and Erech, and Accad,*

and Calneh, in the land of Shinar. 11 <u>Out of that land went</u> <u>forth Asshur, and builded Nineveh</u>, and the city Rehoboth, and Calah, 12 And Resen between Nineveh and Calah: the same is a great city. 13 And Mizraim begat Ludim, and Anamim, and Lehabim, and Naphtuhim, 14 And Pathrusim, and Casluhim, (out of whom came Philistim,) and Caphtorim.[27]

II Kings 18:9 And it came to pass in the fourth year of king Hezekiah, which was the seventh year of Hoshea son of Elah king of Israel, that Shalmaneser king of Assyria came up against Samaria, and besieged it. 10 And at the end of three years they took it: even in the sixth year of Hezekiah, that is in the ninth year of Hoshea king of Israel, Samaria was taken. 11 And the king of Assyria did carry away Israel unto Assyria, and put them in Halah and in Habor by the river of Gozan, and in the cities of the Medes: 12 Because they obeyed not the voice of the LORD their God, but transgressed his covenant, and all that Moses the servant of the LORD commanded, and would not hear them, nor do them.[28]

As we have seen, the relationships of these people groups to Israel is not simply due to their geographical proximity to Israel, but because of ancient hatred. For this reason, the people groups descended from Ham, Esau, Ishmael, and Lot have wrought havoc on the line of Shem, Abraham, Isaac, and Jacob.

To this point, we have discussed the reason for dissent. We have also discussed who the dissenters are. We will now look at what action God is being asked to take against them.

Psalm 83:9-12

Psalm 83:9 Do unto them as unto the Midianites; as to Sisera, as to Jabin, at the brook of Kison: 10 Which perished at Endor: they became as dung for the earth. 11 Make their nobles like Oreb, and like Zeeb: yea, all their princes as Zebah, and as Zalmunna: 12 Who said, Let us take to ourselves the houses of God in possession.[29]

There are a lot of reference points listed above, beginning with the judgments of certain people. Psalm 83:9 refers to two different events, both of which are recorded in the book of Judges. The story of Israel and the Midianites can be found in Judges 6-8. We will begin there.

> *Judges 6:1 And the children of Israel did evil in the sight of the LORD: and the LORD delivered them into the hand of Midian seven years. 2 And the hand of Midian prevailed against Israel: and because of the Midianites the children of Israel made them the dens which are in the mountains, and caves, and strong holds. 3 And so it was, when Israel had sown, that the Midianites came up, and the Amalekites, and the children of the east, even they came up against them; 4 And they encamped against them, and destroyed the increase of the earth, till thou come unto Gaza, and left no sustenance for Israel, neither sheep, nor ox, nor ass. 5 For they came up with their cattle and their tents, and they came as grasshoppers for multitude; for both they and their camels were without number: and they entered into the land to destroy it. 6 And Israel was greatly impoverished because of the Midianites; and the children of Israel cried unto the LORD.[30]*

The Lord's response to Israel's cry was to send them a prophet who reminded them of their continued disobedience, even after God had faithfully delivered them from their oppression in Egypt. Even so, the Lord was going to deliver Israel again. This, He did by the hand of Gideon and 300 men. There were not more than 300, because the

Lord wanted Israel to know He was responsible for their victory; salvation was not wrought by their own hands.

Judges 7:2 And the LORD said unto Gideon, The people that are with thee are too many for me to give the Midianites into their hands, lest Israel vaunt themselves against me, saying, Mine own hand hath saved me. 3 Now therefore go to, proclaim in the ears of the people, saying, Whosoever is fearful and afraid, let him return and depart early from mount Gilead. And there returned of the people twenty and two thousand; and there remained ten thousand. 4 And the LORD said unto Gideon, The people are yet too many; bring them down unto the water, and I will try them for thee there: and it shall be, that of whom I say unto thee, This shall go with thee, the same shall go with thee; and of whomsoever I say unto thee, This shall not go with thee, the same shall not go. 5 So he brought down the people unto the water: and the LORD said unto Gideon, Every one that lappeth of the water with his tongue, as a dog lappeth, him shalt thou set by himself; likewise every one that boweth down upon his knees to drink. 6 And the number of them that lapped, putting their hand to their mouth, were three hundred men: but all the rest of the people bowed down upon their knees to drink water. 7 And the LORD said unto Gideon, By the three hundred men that lapped will I save you, and deliver the Midianites into thine hand: and let all the other people go every man unto his place. 8 So the people took victuals in their hand, and their trumpets: and he sent all the rest of Israel every man unto his tent, and retained those three hundred men: and the host of Midian was beneath him in the valley. 9 And it came to pass the same night, that the LORD said unto him, Arise, get thee down unto the host; for I have delivered it into thine hand. 10 But if thou fear to go down, go thou with Phurah thy servant down to the host: 11 And thou shalt hear what they say; and afterward shall thine hands be strengthened to go down unto the host. Then went he down with Phurah his servant unto the outside of the armed men that were in the host. 12 And the Midianites and the Amalekites and all the children of the east lay along in the valley like grasshoppers

21

for multitude; and their camels were without number, as the sand by the sea side for multitude. 13 And when Gideon was come, behold, there was a man that told a dream unto his fellow, and said, Behold, I dreamed a dream, and, lo, a cake of barley bread tumbled into the host of Midian, and came unto a tent, and smote it that it fell, and overturned it, that the tent lay along. 14 And his fellow answered and said, This is nothing else save the sword of Gideon the son of Joash, a man of Israel: for into his hand hath God delivered Midian, and all the host. 15 And it was so, when Gideon heard the telling of the dream, and the interpretation thereof, that he worshipped, and returned into the host of Israel, and said, Arise; for the LORD hath delivered into your hand the host of Midian. 16 And he divided the three hundred men into three companies, and he put a trumpet in every man's hand, with empty pitchers, and lamps within the pitchers. 17 And he said unto them, Look on me, and do likewise: and, behold, when I come to the outside of the camp, it shall be that, as I do, so shall ye do. 18 When I blow with a trumpet, I and all that are with me, then blow ye the trumpets also on every side of all the camp, and say, The sword of the LORD, and of Gideon. 19 So Gideon, and the hundred men that were with him, came unto the outside of the camp in the beginning of the middle watch; and they had but newly set the watch: and they blew the trumpets, and brake the pitchers that were in their hands. 20 And the three companies blew the trumpets, and brake the pitchers, and held the lamps in their left hands, and the trumpets in their right hands to blow withal: and they cried, The sword of the LORD, and of Gideon. 21 And they stood every man in his place round about the camp; and all the host ran, and cried, and fled. 22 And the three hundred blew the trumpets, and the LORD set every man's sword against his fellow, even throughout all the host: and the host fled to Bethshittah in Zererath, and to the border of Abelmeholah, unto Tabbath.[31]

Thus, the victory was given to Gideon and the Israelites. All the Midianites ran, and cried, and fled when they heard the trumpets, breaking pitchers, and the cry of "The sword of the Lord, and of

Gideon". Those who did not turn their swords upon one another were pursued by men from the tribes of Naphtali, Asher, and Manasseh. The two Midianite princes, Oreb and Zeeb, were slain.

Psalm 83:9 also mentions the following: *as to Sisera, as to Jabin, at the brook of Kison.* The story of this victory is found in Judges 4. As with the previous story, the children of Israel had been taken captive because of their disobedience to the Lord. This time, the Lord used Deborah, Barak, and an army of 10,000 to deliver victory and end the captivity of the Israelites.

> *Judges 4:1 And the children of Israel again did evil in the sight of the LORD, when Ehud was dead. 2 And the LORD sold them into the hand of Jabin king of Canaan, that reigned in Hazor; the captain of whose host was Sisera, which dwelt in Harosheth of the Gentiles. 3 And the children of Israel cried unto the LORD: for he had nine hundred chariots of iron; and twenty years he mightily oppressed the children of Israel. 4 And Deborah, a prophetess, the wife of Lapidoth, she judged Israel at that time. 5 And she dwelt under the palm tree of Deborah between Ramah and Bethel in mount Ephraim: and the children of Israel came up to her for judgment. 6 And she sent and called Barak the son of Abinoam out of Kedeshnaphtali, and said unto him, Hath not the LORD God of Israel commanded, saying, Go and draw toward mount Tabor, and take with thee ten thousand men of the children of Naphtali and of the children of Zebulun? 7 And I will draw unto thee to the river Kishon Sisera, the captain of Jabin's army, with his chariots and his multitude; and I will deliver him into thine hand. 8 And Barak said unto her, If thou wilt go with me, then I will go: but if thou wilt not go with me, then I will not go. 9 And she said, I will surely go with thee: notwithstanding the journey that thou takest shall not be for thine honour; for the LORD shall sell Sisera into the hand of a woman. And Deborah arose, and went with Barak to Kedesh. 10 And Barak called Zebulun and Naphtali to Kedesh; and he went up with ten thousand men at his feet: and Deborah went up with him. 11 Now Heber the Kenite, which was of the children of Hobab the father in law of Moses, had severed*

himself from the Kenites, and pitched his tent unto the plain of Zaanaim, which is by Kedesh. 12 And they shewed Sisera that Barak the son of Abinoam was gone up to mount Tabor. 13 And Sisera gathered together all his chariots, even nine hundred chariots of iron, and all the people that were with him, from Harosheth of the Gentiles unto the river of Kishon. 14 And Deborah said unto Barak, Up; for this is the day in which the LORD hath delivered Sisera into thine hand: is not the LORD gone out before thee? So Barak went down from mount Tabor, and ten thousand men after him. 15 And the LORD discomfited Sisera, and all his chariots, and all his host, with the edge of the sword before Barak; so that Sisera lighted down off his chariot, and fled away on his feet. 16 But Barak pursued after the chariots, and after the host, unto Harosheth of the Gentiles: and all the host of Sisera fell upon the edge of the sword; and there was not a man left.

17 Howbeit Sisera fled away on his feet to the tent of Jael the wife of Heber the Kenite: for there was peace between Jabin the king of Hazor and the house of Heber the Kenite. 18 And Jael went out to meet Sisera, and said unto him, Turn in, my lord, turn in to me; fear not. And when he had turned in unto her into the tent, she covered him with a mantle. 19 And he said unto her, Give me, I pray thee, a little water to drink; for I am thirsty. And she opened a bottle of milk, and gave him drink, and covered him. 20 Again he said unto her, Stand in the door of the tent, and it shall be, when any man doth come and enquire of thee, and say, Is there any man here? that thou shalt say, No. 21 Then Jael Heber's wife took a nail of the tent, and took an hammer in her hand, and went softly unto him, and smote the nail into his temples, and fastened it into the ground: for he was fast asleep and weary. So he died. 22 And, behold, as Barak pursued Sisera, Jael came out to meet him, and said unto him, Come, and I will shew thee the man whom thou seekest. And when he came into her tent, behold, Sisera lay dead, and the nail was in his temples. 23 So God subdued on that day Jabin the king of Canaan before the children of Israel. 24 And the hand of the children of Israel prospered, and prevailed against Jabin the king of Canaan, until they had destroyed Jabin king of Canaan.

As with the story of Gideon, it is important to note victory was given to the Israelites by the hand of the Lord. They did not have to fight for it. In Judges 7, the Lord caused confusion and terror to fall upon the Midianites so they killed each other. In Judges 4:15, we are told the same confusion and terror struck Sisera and his army, and they basically stood there and allowed themselves to be killed by the hand of Barak and the Israelites. There was no real "battle".

Psalm 83:10 tells us Sisera and Jabin died at Endor. Although Judges 4 does not explicitly state this, Judges 5 includes the song of Deborah and Barak and tells us the location of this victory occurred in Taanach by the waters of Megiddo (Judges 5:19), which is by Endor. There, the bodies of the slain were left unburied, as dung upon the earth.

The next verses in Psalm 83 say the following:

> *Psalm 83:11 Make their nobles like Oreb, and like Zeeb: yea, all their princes as Zebah, and as Zalmunna: 12 Who said, Let us take to ourselves the houses of God in possession.*

Oreb and Zeeb were the two Midianite princes slain by the Israelites in Judges 7, after Gideon's victory. Zebah and Zalmunna are found in Judges 8. They were the kings of Midian.

> *Judges 5:4 And Gideon came to Jordan, and passed over, he, and the three hundred men that were with him, faint, yet pursuing them. 5 And he said unto the men of Succoth, Give, I pray you, loaves of bread unto the people that follow me; for they be faint, and I am pursuing after Zebah and Zalmunna, kings of Midian. 6 And the princes of Succoth said, Are the hands of Zebah and Zalmunna now in thine hand, that we should give bread unto thine army? 7 And Gideon said, Therefore when the LORD hath delivered Zebah and Zalmunna into mine hand, then I will tear your flesh with the thorns of the wilderness and with briers. 8 And he went up thence to Penuel, and spake unto them likewise: and the men of Penuel answered him as the men of Succoth had answered*

25

him. *9 And he spake also unto the men of Penuel, saying, When I come again in peace, I will break down this tower. 10 Now Zebah and Zalmunna were in Karkor, and their hosts with them, about fifteen thousand men, all that were left of all the hosts of the children of the east: for there fell an hundred and twenty thousand men that drew sword. 11 And Gideon went up by the way of them that dwelt in tents on the east of Nobah and Jogbehah, and smote the host; for the host was secure. 12 And when Zebah and Zalmunna fled, he pursued after them, and took the two kings of Midian, Zebah and Zalmunna, and discomfited all the host. 13 And Gideon the son of Joash returned from battle before the sun was up, 14 And caught a young man of the men of Succoth, and enquired of him: and he described unto him the princes of Succoth, and the elders thereof, even threescore and seventeen men. 15 And he came unto the men of Succoth, and said, Behold Zebah and Zalmunna, with whom ye did upbraid me, saying, Are the hands of Zebah and Zalmunna now in thine hand, that we should give bread unto thy men that are weary? 16 And he took the elders of the city, and thorns of the wilderness and briers, and with them he taught the men of Succoth. 17 And he beat down the tower of Penuel, and slew the men of the city. 18 Then said he unto Zebah and Zalmunna, What manner of men were they whom ye slew at Tabor? And they answered, As thou art, so were they; each one resembled the children of a king. 19 And he said, They were my brethren, even the sons of my mother: as the LORD liveth, if ye had saved them alive, I would not slay you. 20 And he said unto Jether his firstborn, Up, and slay them. But the youth drew not his sword: for he feared, because he was yet a youth. 21 Then Zebah and Zalmunna said, Rise thou, and fall upon us: for as the man is, so is his strength. And Gideon arose, and slew Zebah and Zalmunna, and took away the ornaments that were on their camels' necks.[32]*

Why were these two kings killed? The answer is in verses 18-19.

18 Then said he unto Zebah and Zalmunna, What manner of men were they whom ye slew at Tabor? And they answered, As thou art, so were they; each one resembled the children of a king. 19 And he said, They were my brethren, even the sons of my mother: as the LORD liveth, if ye had saved them alive, I would not slay you.

This brings to mind Matthew 25's judgment of the sheep and the goats. We will discuss that link in greater detail when we get to Isaiah 17.

One of the predominant viewpoints regarding the potential fulfillment of Psalm 83 is that God will once again use Israel to defeat her enemies. It should be noted Israel played a relatively small role in both victories. God alone was responsible for gathering their enemies and smiting them with terror and confusion so they either killed each other or made it easy for Israel to dispose of them. Israel was not responsible for her victory in either Judges 4 or Judges 7. It should also be noted Israel was being held captive in both cases. Such is not currently the case for Israel. However, there will come a time when captivity will once again be upon them, and they will be delivered out of it. When will this forthcoming captivity occur? During the second half of Daniel's 70th Week.

Daniel 11:31 And arms shall stand on his part, and they shall pollute the sanctuary of strength, and shall take away the daily sacrifice, and they shall place the abomination that maketh desolate. 32 And such as do wickedly against the covenant shall he corrupt by flatteries: but the people that do know their God shall be strong, and do exploits. 33 And they that understand among the people shall instruct many: yet they shall fall by the sword, and by flame, by captivity, and by spoil, many days. 34 Now when they shall fall, they shall be holpen with a little help: but many shall cleave to them with flatteries. 35 And some of them of understanding shall fall, to try them, and to purge, and to make them white, even to the time of the end: because it is yet for a time appointed. 36 And the king shall do according to his will; and he shall exalt himself, and magnify himself above every god, and shall

27

speak marvellous things against the God of gods, and shall prosper till the indignation be accomplished: for that that is determined shall be done. 37 Neither shall he regard the God of his fathers, nor the desire of women, nor regard any god: for he shall magnify himself above all. 38 But in his estate shall he honour the God of forces: and a god whom his fathers knew not shall he honour with gold, and silver, and with precious stones, and pleasant things. 39 Thus shall he do in the most strong holds with a strange god, whom he shall acknowledge and increase with glory: and he shall cause them to rule over many, and shall divide the land for gain.[33]

Will the Lord deliver Israel from the hands of her captors in the same manner as He did in Judges 4 and 7? Indeed, He will.

Zechariah 12:1 The burden of the word of the LORD for Israel, saith the LORD, which stretcheth forth the heavens, and layeth the foundation of the earth, and formeth the spirit of man within him. 2 Behold, I will make Jerusalem a cup of trembling unto all the people round about, when they shall be in the siege both against Judah and against Jerusalem. 3 And in that day will I make Jerusalem a burdensome stone for all people: all that burden themselves with it shall be cut in pieces, though all the people of the earth be gathered together against it. 4 In that day, saith the LORD, I will smite every horse with astonishment, and his rider with madness: and I will open mine eyes upon the house of Judah, and will smite every horse of the people with blindness. 5 And the governors of Judah shall say in their heart, The inhabitants of Jerusalem shall be my strength in the LORD of hosts their God. 6 In that day will I make the governors of Judah like an hearth of fire among the wood, and like a torch of fire in a sheaf; and they shall devour all the people round about, on the right hand and on the left: and Jerusalem shall be inhabited again in her own place, even in Jerusalem. 7 The LORD also shall save the tents of Judah first, that the glory of the house of David and the glory of the inhabitants of Jerusalem do not magnify themselves against Judah. 8 In that day shall the LORD defend the inhabitants of Jerusalem; and he that is feeble among them at that day shall be as David; and the house of David shall be as God, as the angel of the LORD before them. 9 And it shall come to pass in that day, that I will seek to destroy all the nations that come against Jerusalem.[34]

This defeat of Israel's enemies by the hand of the Lord, due to the increase of His strength, will occur at the Second Coming.

Psalm 83:13-18

Psalm 83:13 O my God, make them like a wheel; as the stubble before the wind. 14 As the fire burneth a wood, and as the flame setteth the mountains on fire; 15 So persecute them with thy tempest, and make them afraid with thy storm. 16 Fill their faces with shame; that they may seek thy name, O LORD. 17 Let them be confounded and troubled for ever; yea, let them be put to shame, and perish: 18 That men may know that thou, whose name alone is JEHOVAH, art the most high over all the earth. [35]

Make them as a wheel – from Matthew Poole's Commentary:

> *"or a round ball, which being once tumbled down from the top of a hill, runs down with great force and swiftness, and stays not till it comes to the bottom, and there also is very unstable, and soon removed."* [36]

> *Isaiah 17:13 The nations shall rush like the rushing of many waters: but God shall rebuke them, and they shall flee far off, and shall be chased as the chaff of the mountains before the wind, and like a rolling thing before the whirlwind. 14 And behold at eveningtide trouble; and before the morning he is not. This is the portion of them that spoil us, and the lot of them that rob us.* [37]

As stubble before the wind – from Gill's Exposition of the Entire Bible:

> *"which cannot stand before it, but is driven about by it here and there; and so wicked men are, as chaff and stubble, driven away in their wickedness, with the stormy wind of divine wrath and vengeance, and chased out of the world, which is here imprecated."* [38]

> *Malachi 4:1 For, behold, the day cometh, that shall burn as an oven; and all the proud, yea, and all that do wickedly, shall be stubble: and the day that cometh shall burn them up,*

saith the LORD of hosts, that it shall leave them neither root nor branch.[39]

As the fire burneth a wood, and as the flames setteth the mountains on fire – from Barnes' Notes on the Bible:

> *"No image of desolation is more fearful than that of fire raging in a forest; or of fire on the mountains. As trees and shrubs and grass fall before such a flame, so the prayer is, that they who had combined against the people of God might be swept away by his just displeasure."*[40]

> *Isaiah 64:1 Oh that thou wouldest rend the heavens, that thou wouldest come down, that the mountains might flow down at thy presence, 2 As when the melting fire burneth, the fire causeth the waters to boil, to make thy name known to thine adversaries, that the nations may tremble at thy presence!*[41]

Persecute them with thy tempest, and make them afraid with thy storm – from Barnes' Notes on the Bible.

> *"With the expressions of thy displeasure; with punishment which may be compared with the fury of a storm."*[42]

> *Isaiah 29:6 Thou shalt be visited of the LORD of hosts with thunder, and with earthquake, and great noise, with storm and tempest, and the flame of devouring fire. 7 And the multitude of all the nations that fight against Ariel, even all that fight against her and her munition, and that distress her, shall be as a dream of a night vision. 8 It shall even be as when an hungry man dreameth, and, behold, he eateth; but he awaketh, and his soul is empty: or as when a thirsty man dreameth, and, behold, he drinketh; but he awaketh, and, behold, he is faint, and his soul hath appetite: so shall the multitude of all the nations be, that fight against mount Zion.*[4]

Fill their faces with shame; that they may seek thy name, O Lord. Let them be confounded and troubled for ever; yea, let them be put to shame, and perish: That men may know that thou, whose name alone is JEHOVAH, art the most high over all the earth – from Gill's Exposition of the Entire Bible:

> *"not they themselves, who are filled with shame; for it is imprecated, that they be ashamed, and troubled for ever, and so as to perish, Psalm 83:17 but others; for the words may be supplied, as in Psalm 83:18 "that men may seek thy name, or that thy name may be sought": the judgments of God upon wicked men are sometimes the means of arousing others, and putting them upon seeking the Lord, his face, and his favour; that God would be merciful to them, pardon their iniquities, avert judgments from them, and preserve them from threatened calamities; and this is a good end, when answered; see Isaiah 26:9."[44]*

> *Isaiah 26:4 Trust ye in the LORD for ever: for in the LORD JEHOVAH is everlasting strength: 5 For he bringeth down them that dwell on high; the lofty city, he layeth it low; he layeth it low, even to the ground; he bringeth it even to the dust. 6 The foot shall tread it down, even the feet of the poor, and the steps of the needy. 7 The way of the just is uprightness: thou, most upright, dost weigh the path of the just. 8 Yea, in the way of thy judgments, O LORD, have we waited for thee; the desire of our soul is to thy name, and to the remembrance of thee. 9 With my soul have I desired thee in the night; yea, with my spirit within me will I seek thee early: for when thy judgments are in the earth, the inhabitants of the world will learn righteousness. 10 Let favour be shewed to the wicked, yet will he not learn righteousness: in the land of uprightness will he deal unjustly, and will not behold the majesty of the LORD.[45]*

How can we say for sure the judgments of the people groups listed in Psalm 83 will occur at the Second Coming of Jesus? There are multiple passages of Scripture which reference the final judgments of these specific people groups. Let us begin with the judgment of Edom, since it is listed first.

The Tabernacles of Edom

The judgment of Edom is found in multiple passages in the Old Testament. We will begin with Obadiah. Instead of citing the whole chapter which is entirely pertinent, I will include only specific verses.

Obadiah 1:1 The vision of Obadiah. Thus saith the Lord GOD concerning Edom; We have heard a rumour from the LORD, and an ambassador is sent among the heathen, Arise ye, and let us rise up against her in battle. 2 Behold, I have made thee small among the heathen: thou art greatly despised. 3 The pride of thine heart hath deceived thee, thou that dwellest in the clefts of the rock, whose habitation is high; that saith in his heart, Who shall bring me down to the ground? 4 Though thou exalt thyself as the eagle, and though thou set thy nest among the stars, thence will I bring thee down, saith the LORD.

7 All the men of thy confederacy have brought thee even to the border: the men that were at peace with thee have deceived thee, and prevailed against thee; they that eat thy bread have laid a wound under thee: there is none understanding in him. 8 Shall I not in that day, saith the LORD, even destroy the wise men out of Edom, and understanding out of the mount of Esau? 9 And thy mighty men, O Teman, shall be dismayed, to the end that every one of the mount of Esau may be cut off by slaughter. 10 For thy violence against thy brother Jacob shame shall cover thee, and thou shalt be cut off for ever. 11 In the day that thou stoodest on the other side, in the day that the strangers carried away captive his forces, and foreigners entered into his gates, and cast lots upon Jerusalem, even thou wast as one of them. 12 But thou shouldest not have looked on the day of thy brother in the day that he became a stranger; neither shouldest thou have rejoiced over the children of Judah in the day of their destruction; neither shouldest thou have spoken proudly in the day of distress.

16 For as ye have drunk upon my holy mountain, so shall all the heathen drink continually, yea, they shall drink, and they shall swallow down, and they shall be as though they had not been. 17 But upon mount Zion shall be deliverance, and there shall be holiness; and the house of Jacob shall possess their possessions. 18 And the house of Jacob shall be a fire, and the house of Joseph a flame, and the house of Esau for stubble, and they shall kindle in them, and devour them; and there shall not be any remaining of the house of Esau; for the LORD hath spoken it.

The text of Obadiah includes parallel text from Joel 2, Joel 3, Zechariah 12, Isaiah 63, Amos 1, and Jeremiah 49.

Joel 2:32 And it shall come to pass, that whosoever shall call on the name of the LORD shall be delivered: for in mount Zion and in Jerusalem shall be deliverance, as the LORD hath said, and in the remnant whom the LORD shall call.

Joel 3:1 For, behold, in those days, and in that time, when I shall bring again the captivity of Judah and Jerusalem, 2 I will also gather all nations, and will bring them down into the valley of Jehoshaphat, and will plead with them there for my people and for my heritage Israel, whom they have scattered among the nations, and parted my land. 13 Put ye in the sickle, for the harvest is ripe: come, get you down; for the press is full, the fats overflow; for their wickedness is great. 14 Multitudes, multitudes in the valley of decision: for the day of the LORD is near in the valley of decision. 15 The sun and the moon shall be darkened, and the stars shall withdraw their shining. 16 The LORD also shall roar out of Zion, and utter his voice from Jerusalem; and the heavens and the earth shall shake: but the LORD will be the hope of his people, and the strength of the children of Israel.[46]

Zechariah 12:3 And in that day will I make Jerusalem a burdensome stone for all people: all that burden themselves with it shall be cut in pieces, though all the people of the earth be gathered together against it. 4 In that day, saith the LORD, I will smite every horse with astonishment, and his rider with madness: and I will open mine eyes upon the house of Judah, and will smite every horse of the people with blindness. 5 And the governors of Judah shall say in their heart, The inhabitants of Jerusalem shall be my strength in the LORD of hosts their God. 6 In that day will I make the governors of Judah like an hearth of fire among the wood, and like a torch of fire in a sheaf; and they shall devour all the people round about, on the right hand and on the left: and Jerusalem shall be inhabited again in her own place, even in Jerusalem.

Isaiah 63:1 Who is this that cometh from Edom, with dyed garments from Bozrah? this that is glorious in his apparel, travelling in the greatness of his strength? I that speak in righteousness, mighty to save. 2 Wherefore art thou red in thine apparel, and thy garments like him that treadeth in the winefat? 3 I have trodden the winepress alone; and of the people there was none with me: for I will tread them in mine anger, and trample them in my fury; and their blood shall be sprinkled upon my garments, and I will stain all my raiment. 4 For the day of vengeance is in mine heart, and the year of my redeemed is come.[47]

Amos 1:1 The words of Amos, who was among the herdmen of Tekoa, which he saw concerning Israel in the days of Uzziah king of Judah, and in the days of Jeroboam the son of Joash king of Israel, two years before the earthquake. 2 And he said, The LORD will roar from Zion, and utter his voice from Jerusalem; and the habitations of the shepherds shall mourn, and the top of Carmel shall wither. 11 Thus saith the LORD; For three transgressions of Edom, and for four, I will not turn away the punishment thereof; because he did pursue his brother with the sword, and did cast off all pity, and his anger did tear perpetually, and he kept his wrath for ever: 12 But I will send a fire upon Teman, which shall devour the palaces of Bozrah.[48]

Jeremiah 49:7 Concerning Edom, thus saith the LORD of hosts; Is wisdom no more in Teman? is counsel perished from the prudent? is their wisdom vanished? 8 Flee ye, turn back, dwell deep, O inhabitants of Dedan; for I will bring the calamity of Esau upon him, the time that I will visit him. 9 If grapegatherers come to thee, would they not leave some gleaning grapes? if thieves by night, they will destroy till they have enough. 10 But I have made Esau bare, I have uncovered his secret places, and he shall not be able to hide himself: his seed is spoiled, and his brethren, and his neighbours, and he is not. 13 For I have sworn by myself, saith the LORD, that Bozrah shall become a desolation, a reproach, a waste, and a curse; and all the cities thereof shall be perpetual wastes. 17 Also Edom shall be a desolation: every one that goeth by it shall be astonished, and shall hiss at all the plagues thereof. 18 As in the overthrow of Sodom and Gomorrah and the neighbour cities thereof, saith the LORD, no man shall abide there, neither shall a son of man dwell in it. 19 Behold, he shall come up like a lion from the swelling of Jordan against the habitation of the strong: but I will suddenly make him run away from her: and who is a chosen man, that I may appoint over her? for who is like me? and who will appoint me the time? and who is that shepherd that will stand before me? 20 Therefore hear the counsel of the LORD, that he hath taken against Edom; and his purposes, that he hath purposed against the inhabitants of Teman: Surely the least of the flock shall draw them out: surely he shall make their habitations desolate with them. 21 The earth is moved at the noise of their fall, at the cry the noise thereof was heard in the Red sea. 22 Behold, he shall come up and fly as the eagle, and spread his wings over Bozrah: and at that day shall the heart of the mighty men of Edom be as the heart of a woman in her pangs.[49]

The final destruction of Edom will occur at the Second Coming of Jesus Christ.

Moab

The judgment of Moab is also found in multiple passages in the Old Testament. We will begin with Jeremiah 48. Although the entire chapter is pertinent, I will cite specific verses only.

> *Jeremiah 48:1 Against Moab thus saith the LORD of hosts, the God of Israel; Woe unto Nebo! for it is spoiled: Kiriathaim is confounded and taken: Misgab is confounded and dismayed. 2 There shall be no more praise of Moab: in Heshbon they have devised evil against it; come, and let us cut it off from being a nation. Also thou shalt be cut down, O Madmen; the sword shall pursue thee. 3 A voice of crying shall be from Horonaim, spoiling and great destruction. 4 Moab is destroyed; her little ones have caused a cry to be heard.*
>
> *8 And the spoiler shall come upon every city, and no city shall escape: the valley also shall perish, and the plain shall be destroyed, as the LORD hath spoken. 9 Give wings unto Moab, that it may flee and get away: for the cities thereof shall be desolate, without any to dwell therein.*
>
> *12 Therefore, behold, the days come, saith the LORD, that I will send unto him wanderers, that shall cause him to wander, and shall empty his vessels, and break their bottles. 13 And Moab shall be ashamed of Chemosh, as the house of Israel was ashamed of Bethel their confidence. 14 How say ye, We are mighty and strong men for the war? 15 Moab is spoiled, and gone up out of her cities, and his chosen young men are gone down to the slaughter, saith the King, whose name is the LORD of hosts.*
>
> *20 Moab is confounded; for it is broken down: howl and cry; tell ye it in Arnon, that Moab is spoiled,*
>
> *25 The horn of Moab is cut off, and his arm is broken, saith the LORD. 26 Make ye him drunken: for he magnified himself*

38

against the LORD: Moab also shall wallow in his vomit, and he also shall be in derision.

38 There shall be lamentation generally upon all the housetops of Moab, and in the streets thereof: for I have broken Moab like a vessel wherein is no pleasure, saith the LORD. 39 They shall howl, saying, How is it broken down! how hath Moab turned the back with shame! so shall Moab be a derision and a dismaying to all them about him. 40 For thus saith the LORD; Behold, he shall fly as an eagle, and shall spread his wings over Moab.

42 And Moab shall be destroyed from being a people, because he hath magnified himself against the LORD.[50]

Parallel passages can also be found in Isaiah 15-16, Amos 2, and Zephaniah 2.

Isaiah 16:6 We have heard of the pride of Moab; he is very proud: even of his haughtiness, and his pride, and his wrath: but his lies shall not be so. 7 Therefore shall Moab howl for Moab, every one shall howl: for the foundations of Kirhareseth shall ye mourn; surely they are stricken. 8 For the fields of Heshbon languish, and the vine of Sibmah: the lords of the heathen have broken down the principal plants thereof, they are come even unto Jazer, they wandered through the wilderness: her branches are stretched out, they are gone over the sea. 9 Therefore I will bewail with the weeping of Jazer the vine of Sibmah: I will water thee with my tears, O Heshbon, and Elealeh: for the shouting for thy summer fruits and for thy harvest is fallen. 10 And gladness is taken away, and joy out of the plentiful field; and in the vineyards there shall be no singing, neither shall there be shouting: the treaders shall tread out no wine in their presses; I have made their vintage shouting to cease. 12 Wherefore my bowels shall sound like an harp for Moab, and mine inward parts for Kirharesh. 12 And it shall come to pass, when it is seen that Moab is weary on the high place, that he shall come to his sanctuary to pray; but he shall not

39

prevail. 13 This is the word that the LORD hath spoken
concerning Moab since that time.[51]

Amos 1:1 The words of Amos, who was among the herdmen
of Tekoa, which he saw concerning Israel in the days of
Uzziah king of Judah, and in the days of Jeroboam the son of
Joash king of Israel, two years before the earthquake. 2 And
he said, The LORD will roar from Zion, and utter his voice
from Jerusalem; and the habitations of the shepherds shall
mourn, and the top of Carmel shall wither.

Amos 2:1 Thus saith the LORD; For three transgressions of
Moab, and for four, I will not turn away the punishment
thereof; because he burned the bones of the king of Edom
into lime: 2 But I will send a fire upon Moab, and it shall
devour the palaces of Kirioth: and Moab shall die with
tumult, with shouting, and with the sound of the trumpet:
3 And I will cut off the judge from the midst thereof, and will
slay all the princes thereof with him, saith the LORD.[52]

Zephaniah 2:1 Gather yourselves together, yea, gather
together, O nation not desired; 2 Before the decree bring
forth, before the day pass as the chaff, before the fierce anger
of the LORD come upon you, before the day of the LORD's
anger come upon you. 3 Seek ye the LORD, all ye meek of the
earth, which have wrought his judgment; seek righteousness,
seek meekness: it may be ye shall be hid in the day of the
LORD's anger. 8 I have heard the reproach of Moab, and the
revilings of the children of Ammon, whereby they have
reproached my people, and magnified themselves against
their border. 9 Therefore as I live, saith the LORD of hosts,
the God of Israel, Surely Moab shall be as Sodom, and the
children of Ammon as Gomorrah, even the breeding of
nettles, and saltpits, and a perpetual desolation: the residue
of my people shall spoil them, and the remnant of my people
shall possess them. 10 This shall they have for their pride,
because they have reproached and magnified themselves
against the people of the LORD of hosts. 11 The LORD will be
terrible unto them: for he will famish all gods of the

earth; and men shall worship him, every one from his place, even all the isles of the heathen.[53]

The final destruction of Moab will occur at the Second Coming of Jesus Christ.

Ammon

Continuing along in the same vein, the judgment of Ammon is also found in multiple passages in the Old Testament. We will begin in Jeremiah 49.

> *Jeremiah 49:1 Concerning the Ammonites, thus saith the LORD; Hath Israel no sons? hath he no heir? why then doth their king inherit Gad, and his people dwell in his cities? 2 Therefore, behold, the days come, saith the LORD, that I will cause an alarm of war to be heard in Rabbah of the Ammonites; and it shall be a desolate heap, and her daughters shall be burned with fire: then shall Israel be heir unto them that were his heirs, saith the LORD. 3 Howl, O Heshbon, for Ai is spoiled: cry, ye daughters of Rabbah, gird you with sackcloth; lament, and run to and fro by the hedges; for their king shall go into captivity, and his priests and his princes together. 4 Wherefore gloriest thou in the valleys, thy flowing valley, O backsliding daughter? that trusted in her treasures, saying, Who shall come unto me? 5 Behold, I will bring a fear upon thee, saith the Lord GOD of hosts, from all those that be about thee; and ye shall be driven out every man right forth; and none shall gather up him that wandereth. 6 And afterward I will bring again the captivity of the children of Ammon, saith the LORD.*[54]

Similar passages can also be found in Amos 1 and Zephaniah 2.

> *Amos 1:1 The words of Amos, who was among the herdmen of Tekoa, which he saw concerning Israel in the days of Uzziah king of Judah, and in the days of Jeroboam the son of Joash king of Israel, two years before the earthquake. 2 And he said, The LORD will roar from Zion, and utter his voice from Jerusalem; and the habitations of the shepherds shall mourn, and the top of Carmel shall wither. 13 Thus saith the LORD; For three transgressions of the children of Ammon, and for four, I will not turn away the punishment thereof; because they have ripped up the women with child of Gilead,*

that they might enlarge their border: 14 But I will kindle a fire in the wall of Rabbah, and it shall devour the palaces thereof, with shouting in the day of battle, with a tempest in the day of the whirlwind: 15 And their king shall go into captivity, he and his princes together, saith the LORD.[55]

Zephaniah 2:1 Gather yourselves together, yea, gather together, O nation not desired; 2 Before the decree bring forth, before the day pass as the chaff, before the fierce anger of the LORD come upon you, before the day of the LORD's anger come upon you. 3 Seek ye the LORD, all ye meek of the earth, which have wrought his judgment; seek righteousness, seek meekness: it may be ye shall be hid in the day of the LORD's anger. 8 I have heard the reproach of Moab, and the revilings of the children of Ammon, whereby they have reproached my people, and magnified themselves against their border. 9 Therefore as I live, saith the LORD of hosts, the God of Israel, Surely Moab shall be as Sodom, and the children of Ammon as Gomorrah, even the breeding of nettles, and saltpits, and a perpetual desolation: the residue of my people shall spoil them, and the remnant of my people shall possess them. 10 This shall they have for their pride, because they have reproached and magnified themselves against the people of the LORD of hosts. 11 The LORD will be terrible unto them: for he will famish all the gods of the earth; and men shall worship him, every one from his place, even all the isles of the heathen.[56]

The final destruction of Ammon will occur at the Second Coming of Jesus Christ.

The Philistines and Gaza

There are multiple passages which detail the judgment of the Philistines and of Gaza. Below is a re-post of the map I included at the beginning of this study so you can confirm the Philistines inhabited that land.

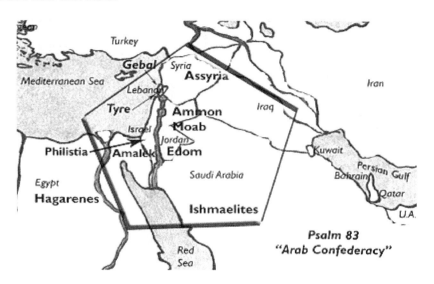

We will begin with the judgment referenced in Jeremiah 47.

> *Jeremiah 47:1 The word of the LORD that came to Jeremiah the prophet against the Philistines, before that Pharaoh smote Gaza. 2 Thus saith the LORD; Behold, waters rise up out of the north, and shall be an overflowing flood, and shall overflow the land, and all that is therein; the city, and them that dwell therein: then the men shall cry, and all the inhabitants of the land shall howl. 3 At the noise of the stamping of the hoofs of his strong horses, at the rushing of his chariots, and at the rumbling of his wheels, the fathers shall not look back to their children for feebleness of hands; 4 Because of the day that cometh to spoil all the Philistines, and to cut off from Tyrus and Zidon every helper that remaineth: for the LORD will spoil the Philistines, the remnant of the country of Caphtor. 5 Baldness is come upon*

Gaza; Ashkelon is cut off with the remnant of their valley:
how long wilt thou cut thyself? 6 O thou sword of the LORD,
how long will it be ere thou be quiet? put up thyself into thy
scabbard, rest, and be still. 7 How can it be quiet, seeing the
LORD hath given it a charge against Ashkelon, and against
the sea shore? there hath he appointed it.[57]

Parallel passages of the destruction of Gaza and of the Philistines
can be found in Amos 1 and Zephaniah 2.

Amos 1:1 The words of Amos, who was among the herdmen
of Tekoa, which he saw concerning Israel in the days of
Uzziah king of Judah, and in the days of Jeroboam the son of
Joash king of Israel, two years before the earthquake. 2 And
he said, The LORD will roar from Zion, and utter his voice
from Jerusalem; and the habitations of the shepherds shall
mourn, and the top of Carmel shall wither. 6 Thus saith the
LORD; For three transgressions of Gaza, and for four, I will
not turn away the punishment thereof; because they carried
away captive the whole captivity, to deliver them up to
Edom: 7 But I will send a fire on the wall of Gaza, which
shall devour the palaces thereof: 8 And I will cut off the
inhabitant from Ashdod, and him that holdeth the sceptre
from Ashkelon, and I will turn mine hand against Ekron: and
the remnant of the Philistines shall perish, saith the Lord
GOD.[58]

Zephaniah 2:1 Gather yourselves together, yea, gather
together, O nation not desired; 2 Before the decree bring
forth, before the day pass as the chaff, before the fierce anger
of the LORD come upon you, before the day of the LORD's
anger come upon you. 3 Seek ye the LORD, all ye meek of the
earth, which have wrought his judgment; seek righteousness,
seek meekness: it may be ye shall be hid in the day of the
LORD's anger. 4 For Gaza shall be forsaken, and Ashkelon a
desolation: they shall drive out Ashdod at the noon day, and
Ekron shall be rooted up. 5 Woe unto the inhabitants of the
sea coast, the nation of the Cherethites! the word of the LORD
is against you; O Canaan, the land of the Philistines, I will

even destroy thee, that there shall be no inhabitant. 6 And the sea coast shall be dwellings and cottages for shepherds, and folds for flocks. 7 And the coast shall be for the remnant of the house of Judah; they shall feed thereupon: in the houses of Ashkelon shall they lie down in the evening: for the LORD their God shall visit them, and turn away their captivity.[59]

The final destruction of the Philistines and Gaza will occur at the Second Coming of Jesus Christ.

Tyre

As with the other land areas and people groups mentioned, the judgment of Tyre is also found in multiple passages. We will begin with Isaiah 23.

> *Isaiah 23:1 The burden of Tyre. Howl, ye ships of Tarshish; for it is laid waste, so that there is no house, no entering in: from the land of Chittim it is revealed to them. 2 Be still, ye inhabitants of the isle; thou whom the merchants of Zidon, that pass over the sea, have replenished. 3 And by great waters the seed of Sihor, the harvest of the river, is her revenue; and she is a mart of nations. 4 Be thou ashamed, O Zidon: for the sea hath spoken, even the strength of the sea, saying, I travail not, nor bring forth children, neither do I nourish up young men, nor bring up virgins. 5 As at the report concerning Egypt, so shall they be sorely pained at the report of Tyre. 6 Pass ye over to Tarshish; howl, ye inhabitants of the isle. 7 Is this your joyous city, whose antiquity is of ancient days? her own feet shall carry her afar off to sojourn. 8 Who hath taken this counsel against Tyre, the crowning city, whose merchants are princes, whose traffickers are the honourable of the earth? 9 The LORD of hosts hath purposed it, to stain the pride of all glory, and to bring into contempt all the honourable of the earth.* [60]

Parallel passages regarding the judgment for Tyre are found in Amos 1 and Joel 3.

> *Amos 1:1 The words of Amos, who was among the herdmen of Tekoa, which he saw concerning Israel in the days of Uzziah king of Judah, and in the days of Jeroboam the son of Joash king of Israel, two years before the earthquake. 2 And he said, The LORD will roar from Zion, and utter his voice from Jerusalem; and the habitations of the shepherds shall mourn, and the top of Carmel shall wither. 9 Thus saith the LORD; For three transgressions of Tyrus, and for four, I will not turn away the punishment thereof; because they delivered*

up the whole captivity to Edom, and remembered not the brotherly covenant: 10 But I will send a fire on the wall of Tyrus, which shall devour the palaces thereof.[61]

Joel 3:1 For, behold, in those days, and in that time, when I shall bring again the captivity of Judah and Jerusalem, 2 I will also gather all nations, and will bring them down into the valley of Jehoshaphat, and will plead with them there for my people and for my heritage Israel, whom they have scattered among the nations, and parted my land. 3 And they have cast lots for my people; and have given a boy for an harlot, and sold a girl for wine, that they might drink. 4 Yea, and what have ye to do with me, O Tyre, and Zidon, and all the coasts of Palestine? will ye render me a recompence? and if ye recompense me, swiftly and speedily will I return your recompence upon your own head; 5 Because ye have taken my silver and my gold, and have carried into your temples my goodly pleasant things: 6 The children also of Judah and the children of Jerusalem have ye sold unto the Grecians, that ye might remove them far from their border. 7 Behold, I will raise them out of the place whither ye have sold them, and will return your recompence upon your own head: 8 And I will sell your sons and your daughters into the hand of the children of Judah, and they shall sell them to the Sabeans, to a people far off: for the LORD hath spoken it. 9 Proclaim ye this among the Gentiles; Prepare war, wake up the mighty men, let all the men of war draw near; let them come up: 10 Beat your plowshares into swords and your pruninghooks into spears: let the weak say, I am strong. 11 Assemble yourselves, and come, all ye heathen, and gather yourselves together round about: thither cause thy mighty ones to come down, O LORD. 12 Let the heathen be wakened, and come up to the valley of Jehoshaphat: for there will I sit to judge all the heathen round about. 13 Put ye in the sickle, for the harvest is ripe: come, get you down; for the press is full, the fats overflow; for their wickedness is great. 14 Multitudes, multitudes in the valley of decision: for the day of the LORD is near in the valley of decision. 15 The sun and the moon shall be darkened, and the stars shall withdraw their shining. 16 The LORD also shall roar out of Zion, and utter his voice from Jerusalem; and the heavens and the earth shall shake: but the LORD will be the hope of his people, and the strength of the children of Israel.[62]

The final destruction of the Tyre will occur at the Second Coming of Jesus Christ.

Concluding Psalm 83

While Psalm 83 does not appear to be its own "conflict", the Lord will most assuredly answer the imprecatory prayer. Each of the passages relating to final destructions link the resolution of the ancient hatred which pitted brother against brother and cousin against cousin to the Second Coming of Jesus Christ.

Perhaps the most substantial link to the Second Coming, which follows pattern more than prophecy, is the idea that Israel was in captivity when the Lord delivered her in both Judges 4 and 7. It was not by her own hand she was delivered, but by the hand of the Lord alone. Thus, the deliverance of the Lord led Israel out of her captivity. For this reason, the link to Zechariah 12 is most important, and Zechariah 12 is a Second Coming chapter. It is also interesting to note text from Daniel 11 which regards the second half of Daniel's 70th Week. I have included additional verses for context, but verse 41 is key.

> *Daniel 11:36 And the king shall do according to his will; and he shall exalt himself, and magnify himself above every god, and shall speak marvellous things against the God of gods, and shall prosper till the indignation be accomplished: for that that is determined shall be done. 37 Neither shall he regard the God of his fathers, nor the desire of women, nor regard any god: for he shall magnify himself above all. 38 But in his estate shall he honour the God of forces: and a god whom his fathers knew not shall he honour with gold, and silver, and with precious stones, and pleasant things. 39 Thus shall he do in the most strong holds with a strange god, whom he shall acknowledge and increase with glory: and he shall cause them to rule over many, and shall divide the land for gain. 40 And at the time of the end shall the king of the south push at him: and the king of the north shall come against him like a whirlwind, with chariots, and with horsemen, and with many ships; and he shall enter into the countries, and shall overflow and pass over. 41 He shall enter also into the glorious land, and many countries shall be*

overthrown: but these shall escape out of his hand, even Edom, and Moab, and the chief of the children of Ammon.[63]

Why do Edom, Moab, and Ammon escape from the hands of the Antichrist? Because Jesus will deal with them Himself at His Second Coming. This fact is detailed in Numbers 24.

Numbers 24:16 He hath said, which heard the words of God, and knew the knowledge of the most High, which saw the vision of the Almighty, falling into a trance, but having his eyes open: 17 I shall see him, but not now: I shall behold him, but not nigh: there shall come a Star out of Jacob, and a Sceptre shall rise out of Israel, and shall smite the corners of Moab, and destroy all the children of Sheth. 18 And Edom shall be a possession, Seir also shall be a possession for his enemies; and Israel shall do valiantly. 19 Out of Jacob shall come he that shall have dominion, and shall destroy him that remaineth of the city.[64]

Many people would differ with my conclusion, and that is perfectly fine. It is up to each person to be like the Bereans and search the scripture for themselves. It is incumbent upon me, however, to include one other prophecy which is linked to each of the final destructions above. It has not been discussed up to this point, because it was not mentioned within the text of Psalm 83. However, the destruction of Damascus is intricately interwoven within the same chapters as have already been referenced, including Jeremiah 49 and Amos 1. Thus, this study would not be complete without discussing the burden of Damascus.

51

The Burden of Damascus

The destruction of Damascus is perhaps one of the most recognized outstanding prophecies of our time. With current events being as they are in the Middle East, and especially in Syria, most people recognize the name Damascus even if they are unaware the destruction of the city is prophetic. Isaiah 17 is an often-quoted passage of Scripture, and it is titled "the burden of Damascus". Below is the text of the chapter.

> *Isaiah 17:1 The burden of Damascus. Behold, Damascus is taken away from being a city, and it shall be a ruinous heap. 2 The cities of Aroer are forsaken: they shall be for flocks, which shall lie down, and none shall make them afraid. 3 The fortress also shall cease from Ephraim, and the kingdom from Damascus, and the remnant of Syria: they shall be as the glory of the children of Israel, saith the LORD of hosts. 4 And in that day it shall come to pass, that the glory of Jacob shall be made thin, and the fatness of his flesh shall wax lean. 5 And it shall be as when the harvestman gathereth the corn, and reapeth the ears with his arm; and it shall be as he that gathereth ears in the valley of Rephaim. 6 Yet gleaning grapes shall be left in it, as the shaking of an olive tree, two or three berries in the top of the uppermost bough, four or five in the outmost fruitful branches thereof, saith the LORD God of Israel. 7 At that day shall a man look to his Maker, and his eyes shall have respect to the Holy One of Israel. 8 And he shall not look to the altars, the work of his hands, neither shall respect that which his fingers have made, either the groves, or the images. 9 In that day shall his strong cities be as a forsaken bough, and an uppermost branch, which they left because of the children of Israel: and there shall be desolation. 10 Because thou hast forgotten the God of thy salvation, and hast not been mindful of the rock of thy strength, therefore shalt thou plant pleasant plants, and shalt set it with strange slips: 11 In the day shalt thou make thy plant to grow, and in the morning shalt thou make thy seed to flourish: but the harvest shall be a heap in the day of*

grief and of desperate sorrow. 12 Woe to the multitude of many people, which make a noise like the noise of the seas; and to the rushing of nations, that make a rushing like the rushing of mighty waters! 13 The nations shall rush like the rushing of many waters: but God shall rebuke them, and they shall flee far off, and shall be chased as the chaff of the mountains before the wind, and like a rolling thing before the whirlwind. 14 And behold at eveningtide trouble; and before the morning he is not. This is the portion of them that spoil us, and the lot of them that rob us.[65]

Parallel passages which relate the destruction of Damascus can be found in Jeremiah 49 and Amos 1.

Jeremiah 49:23 Concerning Damascus. Hamath is confounded, and Arpad: for they have heard evil tidings: they are fainthearted; there is sorrow on the sea; it cannot be quiet. 24 Damascus is waxed feeble, and turneth herself to flee, and fear hath seized on her: anguish and sorrows have taken her, as a woman in travail. 25 How is the city of praise not left, the city of my joy! 26 Therefore her young men shall fall in her streets, and all the men of war shall be cut off in that day, saith the LORD of hosts. 27 And I will kindle a fire in the wall of Damascus, and it shall consume the palaces of Benhadad.[66]

Amos 1:1 The words of Amos, who was among the herdmen of Tekoa, which he saw concerning Israel in the days of Uzziah king of Judah, and in the days of Jeroboam the son of Joash king of Israel, two years before the earthquake. 2 And he said, The LORD will roar from Zion, and utter his voice from Jerusalem; and the habitations of the shepherds shall mourn, and the top of Carmel shall wither. 3 Thus saith the LORD; For three transgressions of Damascus, and for four, I will not turn away the punishment thereof; because they have threshed Gilead with threshing instruments of iron: 4 But I will send a fire into the house of Hazael, which shall devour the palaces of Benhadad. 5 I will break also the bar of Damascus, and cut off the inhabitant from the plain of Aven,

*and him that holdeth the sceptre from the house of Eden: and
the people of Syria shall go into captivity unto Kir, saith the
LORD.*[67]

As with the other prophecies of final destruction, the destruction of
Damascus will occur at the Second Coming of Jesus Christ.

... but it's not really as simple as leaving it at that, is it?
Probably not.

To make this a bit more digestible, we will go through each
verse of the chapter and see exactly what we are being told. As with
Psalm 83, exegesis of Isaiah 17 will be broken up into four parts:
verses 1-2, verses 3-8, verses 9-11, and verses 12-14. We will begin
with Isaiah 17:1-2.

Isaiah 17:1-2

Isaiah 17:1 The burden of Damascus. Behold, Damascus is taken away from being a city, and it shall be a ruinous heap. 2 The cities of Aroer are forsaken: they shall be for flocks, which shall lie down, and none shall make them afraid.

Prophecy scholars understand verse 1 means there will be some type of destruction which will render Damascus desolate. The Hebrew word for "taken away" is "sur" and means "to abolish".[68] Thus, we can know for sure the destruction of one of the world's oldest cities is both final and yet to be fulfilled.

Next, we are told the cities of Aroer will be forsaken or deserted, as well. Their use will be as pasture lands only. There are three different Aroers in the Bible. Per the Benson Commentary, the Aroer mentioned in Isaiah 17:2 is believed to be in the valley between the Lebanon and Anti-Lebanon Mountains, placing it northwest of Damascus.[69] Jeremiah 49 and Amos 1 also mention Hamath, Arpad, Kedar, Hazael, and Benhadad. Below is a map which shows the locations of those ancient areas.

As you can see from the map, quite a widespread area in Syria will be affected, not just the city of Damascus. We are further told no one will make the flocks in these pasture lands afraid. The implication is that they will have no fear because the land will be deserted. The next verses help us understand why the land will be deserted.

Isaiah 17:3 The fortress also shall cease from Ephraim, and the kingdom from Damascus, and the remnant of Syria: they shall be as the glory of the children of Israel, saith the LORD of hosts. 4 And in that day it shall come to pass, that the glory of Jacob shall be made thin, and the fatness of his flesh shall wax lean. 5 And it shall be as when the harvestman gathereth the corn, and reapeth the ears with his arm; and it shall be as he that gathereth ears in the valley of Rephaim. 6 Yet gleaning grapes shall be left in it, as the shaking of an olive tree, two or three berries in the top of the uppermost bough, four or five in the outmost fruitful branches thereof, saith the LORD God of Israel. 7 At that day shall a man look to his Maker, and his eyes shall have respect to the Holy One of Israel. 8 And he shall not look to the altars, the work of his hands, neither shall respect that which his fingers have made, either the groves, or the images.

The fortress also shall cease from Ephraim, and the kingdom from Damascus, and the remnant of Syria –

I have only marginally studied this, but Ephraim is the largest of the 10 tribes in the divided kingdom. Ephraim was allied with Damascus, and will also find herself ruined. The book of Hosea regards the sin of Ephraim and her punishment for it at length. Ephraim's sin was that of idolatry.

Hosea 5:9 Ephraim shall be desolate in the day of rebuke: among the tribes of Israel have I made known that which shall surely be. 10 The princes of Judah were like them that remove the bound: therefore I will pour out my wrath upon them like water. 11 Ephraim is oppressed and broken in judgment, because he willingly walked after the commandment. 12 Therefore will I be unto Ephraim as a moth, and to the house of Judah as rottenness. 13 When Ephraim saw his sickness, and Judah saw his wound, then went Ephraim to the Assyrian, and sent to king Jareb: yet could he not heal you, nor cure you of your wound. 14 For I will be unto Ephraim as a lion, and as a young lion to the house of Judah: I, even I, will tear and go away; I will take away, and none shall rescue him. 15 I will go and return to my place, till they acknowledge their offence, and seek my face: in their affliction they will seek me early.[71]

They shall be as the glory of the children of Israel. The glory of the children of Israel shall be made thin, and the fatness of his flesh shall wax lean –

In attempting to place the timing of the destruction of Damascus, these verses are significant. Currently, Israel is wealthy, secure, and confident in her abilities to defend herself. These are the precise conditions required of Israel for when she is to be attacked by the armies of Gog and Magog. Even so, we know from the text of Ezekiel 38-39 God will save Israel with no assistance from her at all. These conditions of wealth, security, and confidence are the antithesis of what we are told of Israel in Isaiah 17.

For Isaiah 17 to occur before the start of Daniel's 70th Week, Israel would have to be brought to her figurative knees, then built back up to her present-day conditions for the Battle of Gog and Magog to commence. This presupposes there must be more than a few years in between the destruction of Damascus and the Battle of Gog and Magog. In my opinion, that simply does not make sense. Rather, Scripture already tells us of a time when Israel will be brought to her knees. It would make more sense to place the final destruction of Damascus at that time instead of the present day.

Zechariah 13:7 Awake, O sword, against my shepherd, and against the man that is my fellow, saith the LORD of hosts: smite the shepherd, and the sheep shall be scattered: and I will turn mine hand upon the little ones. 8 And it shall come to pass, that in all the land, saith the LORD, two parts therein shall be cut off and die; but the third shall be left therein. 9 And I will bring the third part through the fire, and will refine them as silver is refined, and will try them as gold is tried: they shall call on my name, and I will hear them: I will say, It is my people: and they shall say, The LORD is my God.[72]

It shall be as when the harvestman gathereth the corn, and reapeth the ears with his arm; Yet gleaning grapes shall be left in it, as the shaking of an olive tree, two or three berries in the top of the uppermost bough, four or five in the outmost fruitful branches thereof –

These verses are particularly interesting, because they relate to two different harvests. The gathering of the corn is a reference to grain harvests. We also have a reference to gleaning grapes and olives. Similarly, the end of the world is also compared to those two harvests.

> *Matthew 13:36 Then Jesus sent the multitude away, and went into the house: and his disciples came unto him, saying, Declare unto us the parable of the tares of the field. 37 He answered and said unto them, He that soweth the good seed is the Son of man; 38 The field is the world; the good seed are the children of the kingdom; but the tares are the children of the wicked one; 39 The enemy that sowed them is the devil; the harvest is the end of the world; and the reapers are the angels. 40 As therefore the tares are gathered and burned in the fire; so shall it be in the end of this world. 41 The Son of man shall send forth his angels, and they shall gather out of his kingdom all things that offend, and them which do iniquity; 42 And shall cast them into a furnace of fire: there shall be wailing and gnashing of teeth.[73]*

The end of the world is also likened to the grape harvest.

> *Revelation 14:14 And I looked, and behold a white cloud, and upon the cloud one sat like unto the Son of man, having on his head a golden crown, and in his hand a sharp sickle. 15 And another angel came out of the temple, crying with a loud voice to him that sat on the cloud, Thrust in thy sickle, and reap: for the time is come for thee to reap; for the harvest of the earth is ripe. 16 And he that sat on the cloud thrust in his sickle on the earth; and the earth was reaped. 17 And another angel came out of the temple which is in heaven, he also having a sharp sickle. 18 And another angel*

came out from the altar, which had power over fire; and cried with a loud cry to him that had the sharp sickle, saying, Thrust in thy sharp sickle, and gather the clusters of the vine of the earth; for her grapes are fully ripe. 19 And the angel thrust in his sickle into the earth, and gathered the vine of the earth, and cast it into the great winepress of the wrath of God. 20 And the winepress was trodden without the city, and blood came out of the winepress, even unto the horse bridles, by the space of a thousand and six hundred furlongs.[74]

Revelation 19:11 And I saw heaven opened, and behold a white horse; and he that sat upon him was called Faithful and True, and in righteousness he doth judge and make war. 12 His eyes were as a flame of fire, and on his head were many crowns; and he had a name written, that no man knew, but he himself. 13 And he was clothed with a vesture dipped in blood: and his name is called The Word of God. 14 And the armies which were in heaven followed him upon white horses, clothed in fine linen, white and clean. 15 And out of his mouth goeth a sharp sword, that with it he should smite the nations: and he shall rule them with a rod of iron: and he treadeth the winepress of the fierceness and wrath of Almighty God.[75]

Joel 3:9 Proclaim ye this among the Gentiles; Prepare war, wake up the mighty men, let all the men of war draw near; let them come up: 10 Beat your plowshares into swords and your pruninghooks into spears: let the weak say, I am strong. 11 Assemble yourselves, and come, all ye heathen, and gather yourselves together round about: thither cause thy mighty ones to come down, O LORD. 12 Let the heathen be wakened, and come up to the valley of Jehoshaphat: for there will I sit to judge all the heathen round about. 13 Put ye in the sickle, for the harvest is ripe: come, get you down; for the press is full, the fats overflow; for their wickedness is great. 14 Multitudes, multitudes in the valley of decision: for the day of the LORD is near in the valley of decision. 15 The sun and the moon shall be darkened, and the stars shall withdraw their shining. 16 The LORD also shall roar out of Zion, and utter his voice from Jerusalem; and the heavens and the earth shall shake: but the LORD will be the hope of his people, and the strength of the children of Israel.[76]

The references to gleaning grapes and a few olives left at the tops of the trees are to those Gentiles who will not be destroyed by Jesus at His Second Coming. They will be granted entry into the Millennial Kingdom. The judgment of the sheep and the goats, which is synonymous with the judgment in the valley of decision, affirms this.

Matthew 25:31 When the Son of man shall come in his glory, and all the holy angels with him, then shall he sit upon the throne of his glory: 32 And before him shall be gathered all nations: and he shall separate them one from another, as a shepherd divideth his sheep from the goats: 33 And he shall set the sheep on his right hand, but the goats on the left. 34 Then shall the King say unto them on his right hand, Come, ye blessed of my Father, inherit the kingdom prepared for you from the foundation of the world: 35 For I was an hungred, and ye gave me meat: I was thirsty, and ye gave me drink: I was a stranger, and ye took me in: 36 Naked, and ye clothed me: I was sick, and ye visited me: I was in prison, and ye came unto me. 37 Then shall the righteous answer him, saying, Lord, when saw we thee an hungred, and fed thee? or thirsty, and gave thee drink? 38 When saw we thee a stranger, and took thee in? or naked, and clothed thee? 39 Or when saw we thee sick, or in prison, and came unto thee? 40 And the King shall answer and say unto them, Verily I say unto you, Inasmuch as ye have done it unto one of the least of these my brethren, ye have done it unto me. 41 Then shall he say also unto them on the left hand, Depart from me, ye cursed, into everlasting fire, prepared for the devil and his angels: 42 For I was an hungred, and ye gave me no meat: I was thirsty, and ye gave me no drink: 43 I was a stranger, and ye took me not in: naked, and ye clothed me not: sick, and in prison, and ye visited me not. 44 Then shall they also answer him, saying, Lord, when saw we thee an hungred, or athirst, or a stranger, or naked, or sick, or in prison, and did

*not minister unto thee? 45 Then shall he answer them,
saying, Verily I say unto you, Inasmuch as ye did it not to one
of the least of these, ye did it not to me. 46 And these shall go
away into everlasting punishment: but the righteous into life
eternal.*[77]

That there will be a Gentile remnant spared from the judgments of
the Day of the Lord is also referenced in Isaiah 17:7 –

*At that day shall a man look to his Maker, and his eyes shall
have respect to the Holy One of Israel.*

This idea is parallel to the last several verses of Psalm 83's
imprecatory prayer, specifically verse 18.

*Isaiah 83:13 O my God, make them like a wheel; as the
stubble before the wind. 14 As the fire burneth a wood, and
as the flame setteth the mountains on fire; 15 So persecute
them with thy tempest, and make them afraid with thy storm.
16 Fill their faces with shame; that they may seek thy name,
O LORD. 17 Let them be confounded and troubled for ever;
yea, let them be put to shame, and perish: 18 That men may
know that thou, whose name alone is JEHOVAH, art the most
high over all the earth.*

After all, isn't looking to the Maker, the Holy One of Israel, what the
angel told everyone to do just before the bowls of wrath were poured
out?

*Revelation 14:6 And I saw another angel fly in the midst of
heaven, having the everlasting gospel to preach unto them
that dwell on the earth, and to every nation, and kindred, and
tongue, and people, 7 Saying with a loud voice, Fear God,
and give glory to him; for the hour of his judgment is come:
and worship him that made heaven, and earth, and the sea,
and the fountains of waters.*[78]

And in that day, when the remnant of Gentiles looks to the Maker, the Holy One of Israel, they will cease looking to the altars and images which served their idolatry.

Isaiah 17:9-11

Isaiah 17:9 In that day shall his strong cities be as a forsaken bough, and an uppermost branch, which they left because of the children of Israel: and there shall be desolation. 10 Because thou hast forgotten the God of thy salvation, and hast not been mindful of the rock of thy strength, therefore shalt thou plant pleasant plants, and shalt set it with strange slips: 11 In the day shalt thou make thy plant to grow, and in the morning shalt thou make thy seed to flourish: but the harvest shall be a heap in the day of grief and of desperate sorrow.

In that day shall his strong cities be as a forsaken bough, and an uppermost branch, which they left because of the children of Israel: and there shall be desolation –

> *Isaiah 6:9 And he said, Go, and tell this people, Hear ye indeed, but understand not; and see ye indeed, but perceive not. 10 Make the heart of this people fat, and make their ears heavy, and shut their eyes; lest they see with their eyes, and hear with their ears, and understand with their heart, and convert, and be healed. 11 Then said I, Lord, how long? And he answered, Until the cities be wasted without inhabitant, and the houses without man, and the land be utterly desolate, 12 And the LORD have removed men far away, and there be a great forsaking in the midst of the land. 13 But yet in it shall be a tenth, and it shall return, and shall be eaten: as a teil tree, and as an oak, whose substance is in them, when they cast their leaves: so the holy seed shall be the substance thereof.[79]*

> *Zechariah 12:6 In that day will I make the governors of Judah like an hearth of fire among the wood, and like a torch of fire in a sheaf; and they shall devour all the people round about, on the right hand and on the left: and Jerusalem shall be inhabited again in her own place, even in Jerusalem.[80]*

Because thou hast forgotten the God of thy salvation, and has not been mindful of the rock of thy strength – from Ellicott's Commentary for English Readers:

> *"Jehovah, as the true defence, the fortress rock of His people (Deuteronomy 32:4), is contrasted with the rock-fortresses in which the people had put their trust. They had forsaken the One, and therefore, by a just retribution, the others should be forsaken."*[81]

Therefore shalt thou plant pleasant plants, and shalt set it with strange slips: In the day shalt thou make thy plant to grow, and in the morning shalt thou make thy seed to flourish: but the harvest shall be a heap in the day of grief and of desperate sorrow. – from MacLaren's Expositions:

> *"The original application of these words is to Judah's alliance with Damascus, which Isaiah was dead against. He saw that it would only precipitate the Assyrian invasion, as in fact it did. Judah had forsaken God, and because they had done so, they had gone to seek for themselves delights- alliance with Damascus. The image of planting a garden of pleasures, and 'vine slips of a stranger' refers to sensuous idolatry as well as to the entangling alliance. Then follows a contemptuous description of the rapid growth of this alliance and of the care with which Israel cultivated it. 'In a day thou makest thy plant to grow' {or fencest it}, and next morning it was in blossom, so sedulously had they nursed and fostered it. Then comes the smiting contrast of what it was all for-'A harvest heap in the day of sickness and incurable pain.'"*[82]

And from Commentary Critical and Explanatory on the Whole Bible - Unabridged:

> *"And of desperate sorrow - Israel, instead of trusting in Yahweh, tried to gain a flourishing state of affairs by a league with Syria. But the event, promising though appearances were at first, proved the reverse. It ended in their destruction by Assyria. This is the fact set forth in the*

65

imagery of this verse. The connection of this fragment with what precedes is, notwithstanding the calamities coming on Israel, the people of God shall not be utterly destroyed (Isaiah 6:12-13): the Assyrian spoilers shall perish (Isaiah 17:13-14)."[83]

And how shall it come to pass that the people of God shall not be utterly destroyed, but those who come against them will be?

Isaiah 63:1 Who is this that cometh from Edom, with dyed garments from Bozrah? this that is glorious in his apparel, travelling in the greatness of his strength? I that speak in righteousness, mighty to save. 2 Wherefore art thou red in thine apparel, and thy garments like him that treadeth in the winefat? 3 I have trodden the winepress alone; and of the people there was none with me: for I will tread them in mine anger, and trample them in my fury; and their blood shall be sprinkled upon my garments, and I will stain all my raiment. 4 For the day of vengeance is in mine heart, and the year of my redeemed is come. 5 And I looked, and there was none to help; and I wondered that there was none to uphold: therefore mine own arm brought salvation unto me; and my fury, it upheld me. 6 And I will tread down the people in mine anger, and make them drunk in my fury, and I will bring down their strength to the earth.[84]

Isaiah 17:12-14

Isaiah 17:12 Woe to the multitude of many people, which make a noise like the noise of the seas; and to the rushing of nations, that make a rushing like the rushing of mighty waters! 13 The nations shall rush like the rushing of many waters: but God shall rebuke them, and they shall flee far off, and shall be chased as the chaff of the mountains before the wind, and like a rolling thing before the whirlwind. 14 And behold at eveningtide trouble; and before the morning he is not. This is the portion of them that spoil us, and the lot of them that rob us.

The nations coming against Judah being compared to the rushing of many waters is also referenced in Isaiah 8:

Isaiah 8:7 Now therefore, behold, the Lord bringeth up upon them the waters of the river, strong and many, even the king of Assyria, and all his glory: and he shall come up over all his channels, and go over all his banks: 8 And he shall pass through Judah; he shall overflow and go over, he shall reach even to the neck; and the stretching out of his wings shall fill the breadth of thy land, O Immanuel. 9 Associate yourselves, O ye people, and ye shall be broken in pieces; and give ear, all ye of far countries: gird yourselves, and ye shall be broken in pieces; gird yourselves, and ye shall be broken in pieces.[85]

Compare also to Joel 2, which references the Day of the Lord:

Joel 2:1 Blow ye the trumpet in Zion, and sound an alarm in my holy mountain: let all the inhabitants of the land tremble: for the day of the LORD cometh, for it is nigh at hand; 2 A day of darkness and of gloominess, a day of clouds and of thick darkness, as the morning spread upon the mountains: a great people and a strong; there hath not been ever the like, neither shall be any more after it, even to the years of many generations. 3 A fire devoureth before them; and behind them a flame burneth: the land is as the garden of Eden before them, and behind them a desolate wilderness; yea, and nothing shall escape them. 4 The appearance of them is as the appearance of horses; and as horsemen, so shall they run. 5 Like the noise of chariots on the tops of mountains shall they leap, like the noise of a flame of fire that devoureth the stubble, as a strong people set in battle array. 6 Before their face the people shall be much pained: all faces shall gather blackness. 7 They shall run like mighty men; they shall climb the wall like men of war; and they shall march every one on his ways, and they shall not break their ranks: 8 Neither shall one thrust another; they shall walk every one in his path: and when they fall upon the sword, they shall not be wounded. 9 They shall run to and fro in the city; they shall run upon the wall, they shall climb up upon the houses; they shall enter in at the windows like a thief. 10 The earth shall quake before them; the heavens shall tremble: the sun and the moon shall be dark, and the stars shall withdraw their shining: 11 And the LORD shall utter his voice before his army: for his camp is very great: for he is strong that executeth his word: for the day of the LORD is great and very terrible; and who can abide it?[86]

But the wicked will not succeed.

Joel 3:9 Proclaim ye this among the Gentiles; Prepare war, wake up the mighty men, let all the men of war draw near; let them come up: 10 Beat your plowshares into swords and your pruninghooks into spears: let the weak say, I am strong. 11 Assemble yourselves, and come, all ye heathen, and gather yourselves together round about: thither cause thy mighty ones to come down, O LORD. 12 Let the heathen be wakened, and come up to the valley of Jehoshaphat: for there will I sit to judge all the heathen round about. 13 Put ye in the sickle, for the harvest is ripe: come, get you down; for the press is full, the fats overflow; for their wickedness is great. 14 Multitudes, multitudes in the valley of decision: for the day of the LORD is near in the valley of decision. 15 The sun and the moon shall be darkened, and the stars shall withdraw their shining. 16 The LORD also shall roar out of Zion, and utter his voice from Jerusalem; and the heavens and the earth shall shake: but the LORD will be the hope of his people, and the strength of the children of Israel.[87]

And Zephaniah 3:

> *Zephaniah 3:6 I have cut off the nations: their towers are desolate; I made their streets waste, that none passeth by: their cities are destroyed, so that there is no man, that there is none inhabitant. 7 I said, Surely thou wilt fear me, thou wilt receive instruction; so their dwelling should not be cut off, howsoever I punished them: but they rose early, and corrupted all their doings. 8 Therefore wait ye upon me, saith the LORD, until the day that I rise up to the prey: for my determination is to gather the nations, that I may assemble the kingdoms, to pour upon them mine indignation, even all my fierce anger: for all the earth shall be devoured with the fire of my jealousy.*[88]

Isaiah 17 continues by saying - But God shall rebuke them, and they shall flee far off, and shall be chased as the chaff of the mountains before the wind, and like a rolling thing before the whirlwind. Compare to Psalm 83:

> *Psalm 83:13 O my God, make them like a wheel; as the stubble before the wind. 14 As the fire burneth a wood, and as the flame setteth the mountains on fire; 15 So persecute them with thy tempest, and make them afraid with thy storm. 16 Fill their faces with shame; that they may seek thy name, O LORD. 17 Let them be confounded and troubled for ever; yea, let them be put to shame, and perish:*

And finally, Isaiah 17:14 tells us when this destruction of Damascus and the enemies of Israel will occur.

> *And behold at eveningtide trouble; and before the morning he is not. This is the portion of them that spoil us, and the lot of them that rob us.*

This final destruction of Judah's enemies, of which Damascus and Ephraim are included, will occur in the evening. It will be for a recompense upon the heads of those who divided the land for spoil. The division of the land for spoil occurs at the midpoint of Daniel's 70th Week.

> *Daniel 11:36 And the king shall do according to his will; and he shall exalt himself, and magnify himself above every god, and shall speak marvellous things against the God of gods, and shall prosper till the indignation be accomplished: for that that is determined shall be done. 37 Neither shall he regard the God of his fathers, nor the desire of women, nor regard any god: for he shall magnify himself above all. 38 But in his estate shall he honour the God of forces: and a god whom his fathers knew not shall he honour with gold, and silver, and with precious stones, and pleasant things. 39 Thus shall he do in the most strong holds with a strange god, whom he shall acknowledge and increase with glory: and he shall cause them to rule over many, and shall divide the land for gain.[89]*

The judgment for the division of land is found in Joel 3. It is the judgment of the nations in the valley of decision which will occur at the Jesus's Second Coming.

> *Joel 3:1 For, behold, in those days, and in that time, when I shall bring again the captivity of Judah and Jerusalem, 2 I will also gather all nations, and will bring them down into the valley of Jehoshaphat, and will plead with them there for my people and for my heritage Israel, whom they have scattered among the nations, and parted my land. 3 And they have cast lots for my people; and have given a boy for an harlot, and sold a girl for wine, that they might drink.*

Why it is important to note the destruction of Israel's enemies occurs in the evening?

> *Zechariah 14:1 Behold, the day of the LORD cometh, and thy spoil shall be divided in the midst of thee. 2 For I will gather*

all nations against Jerusalem to battle; and the city shall be taken, and the houses rifled, and the women ravished; and half of the city shall go forth into captivity, and the residue of the people shall not be cut off from the city. 3 Then shall the LORD go forth, and fight against those nations, as when he fought in the day of battle. 4 And his feet shall stand in that day upon the mount of Olives, which is before Jerusalem on the east, and the mount of Olives shall cleave in the midst thereof toward the east and toward the west, and there shall be a very great valley; and half of the mountain shall remove toward the north, and half of it toward the south. 5 And ye shall flee to the valley of the mountains; for the valley of the mountains shall reach unto Azal: yea, ye shall flee, like as ye fled from before the earthquake in the days of Uzziah king of Judah: and the LORD my God shall come, and all the saints with thee. 6 And it shall come to pass in that day, that the light shall not be clear, nor dark: 7 But it shall be one day which shall be known to the LORD, not day, nor night: **but it shall come to pass, that at evening time it shall be light.**[90]

Because it is at evening time the glorious appearing of Jesus Christ will take place.

71

Concluding Psalm 83 and Isaiah 17

I fully understand there are many people who believe Isaiah 17 is the next event on the Biblical prophetic calendar. While I do not agree with that, I do see the progressive worsening of conditions in Syria as a sign of the times and of the lateness of the prophetic hour.

In my opinion, it is most important to understand why the final destructions of all these people groups and land areas will occur. They are the results of Jesus's deliverance of His people and of His making of an end of sins so His Millennial Kingdom can be righteous. After all, He is the Righteous Judge. It will be in His capacity as the Righteous Judge that He will return to deliver Israel and remove all sin from the earth. We must keep in mind the enemies of Israel are not enemies of Israel for Israel's sake. As Psalm 83 tells us, they are enemies of God who are using Israel as a weapon against Him. This, He will cease tolerating at the Second Coming.

> *Isaiah 45:20 Assemble yourselves and come; draw near together, ye that are escaped of the nations: they have no knowledge that set up the wood of their graven image, and pray unto a god that cannot save. 21 Tell ye, and bring them near; yea, let them take counsel together: who hath declared this from ancient time? who hath told it from that time? have not I the LORD? and there is no God else beside me; a just God and a Saviour; there is none beside me. 22 Look unto me, and be ye saved, all the ends of the earth: for I am God, and there is none else. 23 I have sworn by myself, the word is gone out of my mouth in righteousness, and shall not return, That unto me every knee shall bow, every tongue shall swear. 24 Surely, shall one say, in the LORD have I righteousness and strength: even to him shall men come; and all that are incensed against him shall be ashamed. 25 In the LORD shall all the seed of Israel be justified, and shall glory.*[91]

About the Author

Heather lives in Michigan with her son and her cat. She has a Master's degree in Management from Walsh College and is currently employed as an analyst. When not working, she can usually be found at home researching Bible prophecy or with her nose stuck in a book. Heather has a YouTube channel which she uses to teach Bible prophecy. She also conducts routine Bible studies using the "chapter-by-chapter, verse-by verse" methodology. Her YouTube channel is named "Heather R", and she hopes you will stop by and visit sometime.

This is Heather's third self-published work.

References

1 https://www.biblegateway.com/passage/?search=psalm+83&version=KJV

2 http://www.biblestudytools.com/dictionary/asaph/

3 http://www.dictionary.com/browse/imprecatory?s=t

4 https://www.biblegateway.com/passage/?search=II+Corinthians+5&version=KJV

5 https://www.biblegateway.com/passage/?search=Genesis+3%3A15&version=KJV

6 https://www.biblegateway.com/passage/?search=Ezra+2&version=KJV

7 https://www.biblegateway.com/passage/?search=ezekiel+37&version=KJV

8 https://www.biblegateway.com/passage/?search=Joel+2&version=KJV

9 https://www.biblegateway.com/passage/?search=I+Corinthians+15&version=KJV

10 https://www.biblegateway.com/passage/?search=Matthew+23&version=KJV

11 https://www.biblegateway.com/passage/?search=zechariah+13&version=KJV

12 https://www.biblegateway.com/passage/?search=Matthew+24&version=KJV

13 https://www.biblegateway.com/passage/?search=Revelation+12&version=KJV

14 http://somehelpful.info/Prophecy/Israel.html

15 https://www.biblegateway.com/passage/?search=Genesis+25&version=KJV

16 https://www.biblegateway.com/passage/?search=Genesis+27&version=KJV

17 https://www.biblegateway.com/passage/?search=genesis+36&version=KJV

18 https://www.biblegateway.com/passage/?search=Exodus+17%3A8-16&version=KJV

19 https://www.biblegateway.com/passage/?search=genesis+16&version=KJV

20 https://www.biblegateway.com/passage/?search=Genesis+17&version=KJV

21 https://www.biblegateway.com/passage/?search=Genesis+19&version=KJV

22 https://www.biblegateway.com/passage/?search=genesis+10&version=KJV

23 https://www.biblegateway.com/passage/?search=exodus+23&version=KJV

24 https://www.gotquestions.org/Israel-Philistines.html

25 https://www.biblegateway.com/passage/?search=Joshua+13&version=KJV

26 https://www.biblegateway.com/passage/?search=Amos+1&version=KJV

27 https://www.biblegateway.com/passage/?search=genesis+10&version=KJV

28 https://www.biblegateway.com/passage/?search=2%20Kings+18&version=KJV

29 https://www.biblegateway.com/passage/?search=psalm+83&version=KJV

30 https://www.biblegateway.com/passage/?search=judges+6&version=KJV

31 https://www.biblegateway.com/passage/?search=Judges+7&version=KJV

32 https://www.biblegateway.com/passage/?search=Judges+8&version=KJV

33 https://www.biblegateway.com/passage/?search=Daniel+11&version=KJV

34 https://www.biblegateway.com/passage/?search=zechariah+12&version=KJV

35 https://www.biblegateway.com/passage/?search=psalm+83&version=KJV

36 http://biblehub.com/commentaries/psalms/83-13.htm

37 https://www.biblegateway.com/passage/?search=isaiah+17&version=KJV

38 http://biblehub.com/commentaries/psalms/83-13.htm

[39] https://www.biblegateway.com/passage/?search=malachi+4&version=KJV
[40] http://biblehub.com/commentaries/psalms/83-14.htm
[41] https://www.biblegateway.com/passage/?search=isaiah+64&version=KJV
[42] http://biblehub.com/commentaries/psalms/83-15.htm
[43] https://www.biblegateway.com/passage/?search=isaiah+29&version=KJV
[44] http://biblehub.com/commentaries/psalms/83-16.htm
[45] https://www.biblegateway.com/passage/?search=isaiah+26&version=KJV
[46] https://www.biblegateway.com/passage/?search=Joel+3&version=KJV
[47] https://www.biblegateway.com/passage/?search=Isaiah+63&version=KJV
[48] https://www.biblegateway.com/passage/?search=amos+1&version=KJV
[49] https://www.biblegateway.com/passage/?search=Jeremiah+49&version=KJV
[50] https://www.biblegateway.com/passage/?search=Jeremiah+48&version=KJV
[51] https://www.biblegateway.com/passage/?search=isaiah+16&version=KJV
[52] https://www.biblegateway.com/passage/?search=Amos+2&version=KJV
[53] https://www.biblegateway.com/passage/?search=zephaniah+2&version=KJV
[54] https://www.biblegateway.com/passage/?search=jeremiah+49&version=KJV
[55] https://www.biblegateway.com/passage/?search=Amos+1&version=KJV
[56] https://www.biblegateway.com/passage/?search=zephaniah+2&version=KJV
[57] https://www.biblegateway.com/passage/?search=jeremiah+47&version=KJV
[58] https://www.biblegateway.com/passage/?search=Amos+1&version=KJV
[59] https://www.biblegateway.com/passage/?search=Zephaniah+2&version=KJV
[60] https://www.biblegateway.com/passage/?search=isaiah+23&version=KJV
[61] https://www.biblegateway.com/passage/?search=Amos+1&version=KJV
[62] https://www.biblegateway.com/passage/?search=joel+3&version=KJV
[63] https://www.biblegateway.com/passage/?search=daniel+11&version=KJV
[64] https://www.biblegateway.com/passage/?search=Numbers+24&version=KJV
[65] https://www.biblegateway.com/passage/?search=Isaiah+17&version=KJV
[66] https://www.biblegateway.com/passage/?search=Jeremiah+49&version=KJV
[67] https://www.biblegateway.com/passage/?search=Amos+1&version=KJV
[68] http://biblehub.com/hebrew/5493.htm
[69] http://biblehub.com/commentaries/isaiah/17-2.htm
[70] https://isthatinthebible.wordpress.com/2015/09/20/canaanites-amorites-and-hittites-in-history-and-the-bible/
[71] https://www.biblegateway.com/passage/?search=Hosea+5&version=KJV
[72] https://www.biblegateway.com/passage/?search=zechariah+13&version=KJV
[73] https://www.biblegateway.com/passage/?search=Matthew+13&version=KJV
[74] https://www.biblegateway.com/passage/?search=revelation+14&version=KJV
[75] https://www.biblegateway.com/passage/?search=revelation+19&version=KJV
[76] https://www.biblegateway.com/passage/?search=joel+3&version=KJV
[77] https://www.biblegateway.com/passage/?search=matthew+25&version=KJV
[78] https://www.biblegateway.com/passage/?search=Revelation+14&version=KJV
[79] https://www.biblegateway.com/passage/?search=isaiah+6&version=KJV
[80] https://www.biblegateway.com/passage/?search=zechariah+12&version=KJV
[81] http://biblehub.com/commentaries/isaiah/17-10.htm
[82] http://biblehub.com/commentaries/isaiah/17-10.htm

[83] https://www.studylight.org/commentary/isaiah/17-11.html
[84] https://www.biblegateway.com/passage/?search=Isaiah+63&version=KJV
[85] https://www.biblegateway.com/passage/?search=Isaiah+8&version=KJV
[86] https://www.biblegateway.com/passage/?search=Joel+2&version=KJV
[87] https://www.biblegateway.com/passage/?search=Joel+3&version=KJV
[88] https://www.biblegateway.com/passage/?search=zephaniah+3&version=KJV
[89] https://www.biblegateway.com/passage/?search=Daniel+11&version=KJV
[90] https://www.biblegateway.com/passage/?search=zechariah+14&version=KJV
[91] https://www.biblegateway.com/passage/?search=isaiah+45&version=KJV

Printed in Great Britain
by Amazon

31865240R00046